D1216786

THE
LAST
HUNDRED
YEARS
Household
Technology

THE LAST HUNDRED YEARS

Household Technology

BY DANIEL COHEN

M. EVANS AND COMPANY, INC. New York

The author and publisher gratefully acknowledge the following for material used in this book.

Excerpts from *A Streak of Luck: The Life and Legend of Thomas Alva Edison* by Robert Conot. Copyright © 1978 by Robert Conot. Reprinted by permission of Seaview Books.

Excerpts from *1929: America Before the Crash* by Warren Sloat. Copyright © 1979 by Warren Sloat. Reprinted by permission of Macmillan Publishing Company, Inc.

Excepts from *Building the Dream: A Social History of Housing in America* by Gwendolyn Wright. Copyright © 1981 by Gwendolyn Wright. Reprinted by permission of Pantheon Books, a Division of Random House, Inc.

Library of Congress Cataloging in Publication Data

Cohen, Daniel.
　　The last 100 years, household technology.

　　Bibliography: p.
　　Includes index.
　　Summary: Describes the evolution of inventions which have lightened household drudgery, and includes a look at gadgets that didn't catch on and also at future possibilities.
　　1. Household appliances—United States—History—Juvenile literature. 2. Technology—United States—History—Juvenile literature. [1. Household appliances—History. 2. Technology—History. 3. Inventions—History] I. Title. II. Title: Last hundred years, household technology.

TX298.C58　1982　683'.3　82-15442

ISBN 0-87131-386-3

Copyright © 1982 by Daniel Cohen
Illustrations © 1982 by M. Evans and Company, Inc.

M. Evans and Company, Inc.
216 East 49 Street
New York, New York 10017

Design by Diane Gedymin
Manufactured in the United States of America

9 8 7 6 5 4 3 2 1

For my grandmother, who was no stranger to the washboard

Contents

1

One Hundred Years Ago

MORNING IN A New York City brownstone, the home of the Imaginary family—one hundred years ago.

The alarm clock rings, and the family begins to stir. Mr. Imaginary puts on his slippers, wraps himself in his robe, and stumbles sleepily down into the cellar to perform his first, and in some respects most difficult, domestic task of the day. While cold and still half asleep he must rattle the furnace grate to shake out the ashes and then shovel in new coals to warm the house.

That job out of the way, he then climbs the stairs to the bathroom, lights the fire under the water heater, dresses while the water heats up, and then begins to shave. He has to shave rapidly, for the children are already clamoring to get into the bathroom. It's the only bathroom in the house.

By this time the maid, an immigrant girl from Ireland, has arrived, and she lights the fire in the kitchen stove in preparation for making breakfast—cooked cereal for the children, cereal, eggs, and muffins for the parents. Then it is off to school for the children. The younger child, a girl, walks to her grammar school; the older boy takes a short trolley ride to his high school. Father too takes the trolley to work downtown.

With the rest of the family gone, it is Mrs. Imaginary's task to take care of all the domestic arrangements. The maid does most of the heavy work, dusting the furniture, airing the beds, and going over the carpets with the family's newly purchased carpet sweeper, a great improvement over the broom, which just seemed to scatter dust.

Mrs. Imaginary's first big task is to see to the laundry, gathering it in bundles, for this is the day that the man from the steam laundry makes his pickup. The laundry man also delivers a bundle of clean laundry. Looking at the newly washed laundry is always an awful moment for Mrs. Imaginary. As usual, sheets have been shredded, possibly beyond repair. There are the customary missing buttons, and one of Mr. Imaginary's dress shirts is missing altogether. It is almost bad enough, Mrs. Imaginary thinks, to make one long for the old-fashioned washboard. But then she smiles at such a ridiculous thought and dismisses it from her mind.

There are a whole stream of other deliveries that day. The milk, bread, and ice wagons all stop at the house. In the warmer months the vegetable man often comes with a selection of produce grown just outside of the city. In the winter there are occasional calls by the coal man, though the family tries to keep a good supply in the cellar at all times. Mrs. Imaginary always hates coal deliveries because afterward everything in the house is covered with a layer of coal dust.

Meats have to be purchased from the butcher along with a few other staple food products from other stores. Mrs. Imaginary decides to do the shopping herself; she likes to keep her eye on the butcher when he weighs the order. She suspects he sometimes weighs his thumb along with the chops. Some of her friends prefer to use their new telephones to call the market and have their orders sent directly to their home. But Mrs. Imaginary always feels that her doing that would be shirking her duty—she knows her attitude is a bit old-fashioned. When it comes to bread, she even bakes her own, some of the time.

Several hours of Mrs. Imaginary's day are devoted to sewing—trying to repair the ravages done to the family linens by the steam laundry and making a school dress for her daughter. She thumbs through the latest Montgomery Ward mail-order catalog, carefully reading the descriptions of the fabrics. Many of her friends have recommended catalog shopping, but she still prefers to go to the stores where she can actually see the goods before buying them. Still, the prices in the catalog are so much better she is sorely tempted. Perhaps in the spring she will order fabrics through the mail and see how it works out, she thinks.

The maid on her endless round of chores brings up more coal from the cellar to heat the stove for cooking dinner. The children return home from school. Along with her regular homework, the daughter spends an hour practicing the piano. A few hours later, Mr. Imaginary himself is home from the day's business. As it gets dark, gas lamps are lit and dinner is served. After dinner, the hard-working and now thoroughly exhausted maid finishes up the dishes and returns by streetcar to her own home, a tenement building far downtown.

On this particular evening, everybody in the Imaginary family stays home. The family retires to the living room, where the daughter plays, or rather tries to play, two newly learned piano pieces. Afterward, the children amuse themselves with the stereoscope before going to bed. Mr. Imaginary retires to his den where he can smoke his cigar in peace and read the rest of the newspaper. Mrs. Imaginary continues to busy herself with sewing.

As bedtime approaches, the gas lamps are lowered, and Mr. Imaginary descends into the cellar for his last major household task of the day, banking the furnace for the night, so that coal will not be wasted.

The Imaginarys were, of course, an imaginary family living in New York City one hundred years ago. I hesitate to say that they were typical, for then as now, there was really no such thing as a typical or average family. For one thing, the Imaginary family was urban at a time when most families in America still lived on farms. They were fairly well-to-do. The family could afford to have a servant; Mrs. Imaginary did not have to become one. But the family was not one of the rich whose needs were attended to by a staff of servants. Mrs. Imaginary did her own sewing and her own marketing, and on some occasions she would do her own cooking and heavy cleaning as well. But she would never have stooped to the horrible task of doing the family washing.

A family like the Imaginarys had a lot of "modern conveniences" of their day. While Mr. Imaginary may have found feeding the furnace first thing in the morning an irksome task, his counterpart on the farm would have had to start the day by putting wood or coal in the room stove or fireplace, just as people had done for centuries. There is no doubt that our urban family was a good deal warmer and more comfortable.

Then Mr. Imaginary went upstairs to shave—in the bathroom. Out on the farm there was no bathroom. On the farm, Pa shaved in his bedroom with water heated on the kitchen stove and brought to the bedroom in a pitcher. There was no bathroom sink in the farmhouse, no bathtub, and no toilet. The farm family used an outdoor privy and chamber pots. The farm family had heard of indoor plumbing, but it somehow seemed unsanitary to them. Even in the Imaginary urban house, the bathroom was a recent addition. It had been converted from a bedroom and thus was much larger than the bathrooms we are used to seeing today. The hot-water heater for the bathroom was right in the room, and it had to be turned up every morning in order to heat even enough water for shaving.

The kitchen of the Imaginary urban house didn't differ in any significant respects from the typical farm kitchen, except that it had a sink with running water, rather than a single pump. The Imaginary house still used a coal-burning cooking stove, though if it had been truly modern it might have had a gas range. Both city and farmhouse had iceboxes. The Imaginary family replaced theirs with a refrigerator around the turn of the century. The farmhouse still had an icebox in 1936.

There were some other obvious differences between the urban house and that of the farm family—the use of gaslights, for example. The city house had it, the farmhouse

Farm family in the kitchen one hundred years ago. (New York Public Library Picture Collection)

did not. But gaslighting didn't extend to all the rooms in the Imaginary house, and there were still plenty of kerosene lamps to be used for darkened corridors and bedrooms and for the times when the gaslights went out, which was fairly often.

Mrs. Imaginary sent her washing out to the steam laundry—a fairly prosperous farm woman might also have sent her washing out, but to a laundress, who did the job with a tub and washboard. But typically, the farm family and the poorer urban families did their own washing.

Women devoted at least one dreary day a week—tradition-ally Monday—to the task of washing the family clothes and linens either in a tub or sink with a washboard or in a hand-powered washing machine. Another day had to be spent ironing what was washed, and in summer that was pure hell. No wonder Mrs. Imaginary was unwilling to abandon the commercial steam laundry, no matter how badly it shredded the family clothes and linens.

On the farm, the family either grew and canned its own food or carefully stored large quantities of what had to be purchased. Shopping was no easy task, for although town was only a few miles away, the trip took all day in a horse-drawn wagon. In the city, marketing was usually every day—and many of the merchants, like the milkman and the breadman, came right to the door. The others would deliver on order. But then the city house didn't really have many facilities for storing perishable foods. In the warmer months, milk would go bad in a day or two even in the icebox.

There was not as much cooking done in city kitchens as in country ones. Not only did people tend to eat lighter meals, they were not at home as much. During the week, men ate their lunches at work, the children in school.

While Mrs. Imaginary had a servant to do the heavy work and some new labor-saving devices like the carpet sweeper, she still had plenty to do in the house—particularly in the area of sewing.

Evening home entertainment in city and country tended to be simple. The farm family was less likely to have a piano and more likely to make music with a guitar or banjo, that is, if anybody had the energy left to stay up much beyond dinner.

By comparing our New York Imaginary family of one hundred years ago with a farm family of that same era, we were looking backward. The farm family lived much the same way as people had in even earlier times. Now let's look forward and compare the home life of Mr. and Mrs. Imaginary and their family with life today, in your home, for example.

One of the biggest differences, though not the most obvious, is the servant. One hundred years ago it was quite possible for an ordinary middle-class family to have at least one full-time servant who came in daily to do most of the heavy work. Servants, even part-time servants, are a comparative rarity today. In fact, even one hundred years ago servants were less common in America than in Europe. In Britain, there was a whole class of people who went "into service," that is, became servants. It was a way of life —practically every family from that of a duke to that of a shopkeeper had at least one servant. The poor, of course, may have become servants, but in any case could not afford them.

Americans have never been entirely comfortable with the idea of having servants or becoming them. Servants were most often immigrants who could find no other work. They treated domestic service as a way up and out of poverty, rather than as a lifetime career. The number of servants has declined sharply over the last one hundred years.

Without servants the woman of the house had to do her own housework—a career of full-time drudgery a century ago. The "servantless household" created a great demand for "labor saving" improvements, fabrics and furniture that were easy to clean, stoves from which the ashes did not have to be carried, machines to wash clothes and dishes, and much, much more. Most of the changes in household technology over the past century were pioneered in America.

Another great but not obvious difference between the home of the Imaginary family and your own is electricity. You have it, the Imaginary family did not. Not only didn't they have electric lights, they didn't have any of the scores of other home appliances that require electricity. The use of electricity is so pervasive a part of our daily lives today that we often don't recognize how important it is until the power goes out. Then, quite suddenly it seems as if everything in the house from the clock to the stove is utterly useless. We go scrambling for candles and flashlights and consider ourselves horribly inconvenienced if the electricity is out for even an hour. One hundred years ago there was no electricity at all in the home.

The Imaginary family had indoor plumbing, hot and cold running water, and a flush toilet. Most people one hundred years ago had none of this. Today it is possible for a teenager to shower and wash his or hair at least once a day. A century ago, the weekly bath was considered adequate, and many people bathed much less often, particularly in the cold weather. In houses without hot and cold running water, the heating and hauling of water was a time-consuming and tedious job.

When was the last time your father went down into the cellar to put coal in the furnace or your mother cleaned the grate in the coal stove? When is the last time you had coal delivered to your house? The coal-fired furnace and the coal-cooking stove have been replaced. There has, however, been a slight resurgence in the use of the wood stove for heating rooms.

Do you spend the evening looking at the stereoscope? Do you even know what a stereoscope is? In the evening, you are likely to switch on the television set. There wasn't any television one hundred years ago, no radio or phonograph either. And you couldn't go to the movies because there weren't any of them. Magazines and newspapers had pictures, but they were drawings not photographs. One hundred years ago photographs could not be reproduced for printing.

When you need clothes today you go to the store and buy them. One hundred years ago most women's and girls' clothes were made at home. What was called "ready to wear" was mainly men's and boys' clothes or specialty items like fancy underwear.

Most of us would find the home of one hundred years ago a difficult and uncomfortable place in which to live. Yet it was a lot better than what had gone before.

In the chapters that follow, we are going to trace the changes that have taken place in the home over the last one hundred years. Nostalgia, which is always popular, is a yearning or pining for the good old days. Nostalgia casts a sort of soothing fog over the events of the past. It is a fog that obscures all sort of unpleasantness—things like the washboard, the coal scuttle or pail, and the outhouse. No one in his or her right mind gets nostalgic about outhouses—but they once were an important part of life.

Nostalgia puts us before a roaring fireplace on a frosty evening, but fails to fill in the detail that while our face is toasty warm, our rear end is ice cold.

Modern family in their "home entertainment center." (Sony Corporation of America)

In our nostalgic view of the past we are living in a large house surrounded by well-trained servants. In reality, it is just as likely that we would have been one of the servants, crawling into bed in a tiny cramped room after a ten- or twelve-hour day of doing the master's dirty work. Or we might have to take the late-night trolley back to our home in the slums and be prepared to be at work again in the early morning.

People one hundred years ago were not satisfied with the way they lived. They were passionate for change. And they did change things. The changes in day-to-day life in the house have been faster and more radical during the past century than during any other time in history.

There have been some losses because of these changes. Since any form of music can be brought directly into our living rooms, we are less likely to learn how to make our own music. And there have been some dubious gains

—the frozen dinner is convenient to prepare but not very good to eat. In general, however, the changes have been highly beneficial. They have to a great degree eliminated the need for servants or for women to be full-time domestic slaves to their own homes. They have made life lighter, cleaner, and more comfortable than it had ever been before.

Sometimes in the desire for change, we didn't count the cost. We became monster consumers of energy. At first that didn't seem to matter, for energy supplies appeared boundless, but now we are beginning to run out of the easy energy sources. The energy sources left are at present expensive and sometimes dangerous. The amount of trash and garbage we produce has multiplied unbelievably, and we are having trouble finding places to put it all. While we can all acknowledge the benefits of change, because of the problems we are a bit less enthusiastic about it than people were one hundred years ago.

Now let's take a closer look and see how some of those changes in the home and the problems they have created came about.

2

The Kitchen

THE WHOLE FAMILY gathered together around the dinner table—it is one of those enduring images of domestic life in America. In this day of frozen dinners and fast-food joints, we often look back nostalgically on family dinners of the past as something good in life that has been lost. Distance lends charm, and the charming picture of the family dinner ignores the unpleasant reality that the dinner had to be cooked, and often that task wasn't charming at all. And when dinner was over, the dishes had to be washed. There is no charm in washing dishes.

About a century ago, there was a determined effort in America to get rid of family dining altogether because preparing food for the family was just too much trouble. A more efficient method of preparing food seemed at hand. A new type of building was going up in the higher-priced neighborhoods of New York and Chicago—the apartment hotel. It was not a place for transients, but a place where families—wealthy families to be sure—could live permanently.

The exclusive and expensive Grosvenor Apartments in New York City provided tenants with two choices for meals, writes Gwendolyn Wright:

> [T]hey could descend to the elegant main dining room on the first floor, or they could have their waiter bring up food on the staff elevator. He would serve piping hot or perfectly chilled dishes in the apartment's private dining room. Then, at the end of the meal he would whisk away the dirty dishes to the kitchen scullery below. . . . It was possible to do away with many of the smells, sounds, and wasted space of household drudgery.

Apartment hotels like the Grosvenor were only for the wealthy, but the innovation of a communal kitchen and other communal facilities in an apartment building seemed promising, and an article in *Scribner's Magazine* declared: "How far space could be economized, and the general wholesomeness of the entire building increased by the abandonment of private kitchens, and the cooking of all food in one place, is a matter yet untested among people of moderate means." Turn-of-the-century utopian novels often envisioned a future in which household drudgery like cooking was confined to a single area of a large apartment building. To the utopian novelists, the good life of the future was to be lived in a world filled with Grosvenor Apartments.

Elegant apartment hotels with centralized kitchens continued to be built into the twentieth century. But for people of moderate means, the concept was never really tried out, and ultimately it faded even for the well-to-do.

For those of moderate means, there was another way to avoid cooking, the boardinghouse. It was most often a large house, usually one that had once been a private home. It was split up into single rooms, and guests shared dinners in a common dining room. One of the ironclad boardinghouse rules was "No cooking in the rooms." Guests paid for room and board, as a package deal.

The boardinghouse was a necessity for young couples who were just starting out and didn't have enough money to buy their own homes. And the boardinghouse was a place for old people, widows, widowers, and others who didn't have a family to take care of them. Common wisdom held that the boardinghouse was "for the newly wed or the nearly dead." But anybody who was single or any couple of limited means, particularly those who had just moved into an area, might find themselves in a boardinghouse, eating whatever fare it was that the board-inghouse owner chose to provide. The boardinghouse was not looked upon as the wave of the future. Most people wanted to get out of them and into their own homes as quickly as possible.

For the private home, and even for the apartment, the kitchen was often the center—the most important room in the house. In Europe, particularly in England, even modest middle-class homes had servants who did much of the cooking and all of the dishwashing for the family. In the United States, the use of servants was never as widespread except in the South where freed black slaves formed a pool of cheap domestic labor. Blacks and recent immigrants have always made up the bulk of servants in the United States. Being a servant is a job most don't take if they can get anything else. The percentage of households in America that had servants dropped steadily throughout the nineteenth century. There is something about being a servant, or even having one, that runs counter to America's vision of itself.

Harriet Beecher Stowe, author of *Uncle Tom's Cabin*, the influential antislavery novel, had some thoughts about servants as well, and with her sister Catharine E. Beecher, she wrote a book on domestic economy, entitled *American Woman's Home*. The revised version contains this observation about domestic service: "Every human being stands (according to the Declaration of Independence) on the same level. . . . There are no hereditary titles, no monopolies, no privileged classes. . . . All are to be free to rise and to fall as the waves of the sea. . . . The condition of domestic service, however, still retains about it something of the influence from feudal times." The "servantless house" became the standard in America.

Without servants, the kitchen was the exclusive kingdom of the woman of the house—or was it her prison? —it was sometimes hard to tell. Cooking and cleaning up afterward were such enormously time-consuming tasks that many women had little time or energy left for anything else. Feminism or the women's liberation movement is not something that began in the 1960s and 1970s. It really began in the nineteenth century. Early feminist leaders realized that the first thing women had to be liberated from was the endless drudgery of the kitchen. Never mind all those nostalgic notions about Grandma happily spending day after day in the kitchen happily putting up preserves and making pies. The nostalgic picture omits scenes of Grandma shoveling coal into the stove or lugging water from the pump to wash the plates. Most of the time kitchen work was sheer unrewarding drudgery—and unnecessary drudgery as well.

The first move toward liberating the woman from at least a measure of kitchen labor was to improve the organization of the kitchen. The typical home kitchen a century ago was a sprawling haphazard affair. A huge stove lurked at one side. Provisions were stored in a pantry a considerable distance from where they were to be used, which might be on an oilcloth-covered table a long way from the stove.

To reformers this randomness seemed horribly wasteful. In the kitchen on a train or in a ship's galley, food storage and preparation were done efficiently in a remarkably limited space. Others looked to the success of the factory system and mass production. Time and motion studies on the assembly line had improved the efficiency of factory work. Attempts were made to apply the same sort of planning and study to household work, particularly work in the kitchen. Christine Frederick, one of the apostles of household efficiency, wrote in *Ladies' Home Journal,* "Didn't I with hundreds of women stoop unnecessarily over kitchen tables, sinks and ironing boards, as well as bricklayers over bricks." By analyzing her movements she found that she had made eighty extra motions in dishwashing alone, and much more effort was wasted in "sorting, wiping and laying away." Frederick complained, "Do we not waste time by walking in poorly arranged kitchens?"

So attempts were made to bring a factorylike rationality to the disorderly field of housework. Phrases like

Small electric wall range for apartments in 1927. (New York Public Library Picture Collection)

"home economics," "domestic science," and "household engineering" began to enter the language.

In reality, housework was never "rationalized" in the way that factory work was, but there were successful efforts to make it more orderly. The efforts were most successful in redesigning the kitchen by viewing it not simply as a collection of appliances and surfaces, but as a unit—a place where a job had to be done quickly and with as much ease as possible. Houses built or remodeled right after World War I tended to feature efficiency kitchens—stove, sink, cabinets, and work surfaces all squeezed into a very small space. Sometimes there was an attached "breakfast nook," a small easy-to-clean area where breakfast or a light lunch could be eaten. Dinner was still to be served in the more traditional dining room. While the "eat in" kitchen, that is, the kitchen with a large table where the family ate most of its meals, was still very common in the American home, it was not considered "modern" or "efficient" by the 1920s.

In order for kitchens to be made more efficient, kitchen appliances had to be modernized—starting with the stove. The typical cooking stove of a century ago was made of cast iron or steel and was a wood- or coal-burning monstrosity. The fuel had to be fed into it by hand. And afterward it had to be cleaned and the ashes carried away. Temperatures in such a stove were hard to regulate, it needed constant tending, and the difficulties in keeping a kitchen clean when coal or firewood and ashes had to be carried through it regularly can easily be imagined.

Even a century ago the solution to the stove problem was already at hand—the gas-heated stove. People had been reasonably quick to accept gas in the gaslight as a source of illumination. But the idea of using gas for cooking encountered a great deal of resistance. Gas cooking stoves of one sort or another had been shown in industrial expositions as early as 1850, and they had seen limited use in hotel or other institutional kitchens. But in 1889 a manufacturer of gas stoves in Chicago complained in his catalog, "For eight years we have been manufacturing Jewel [a gas stove]. We were among the first to appreciate that gas was to be the fuel of the future. Is the use of gas for cooking purposes an extraordinary luxury? No, it is an economical necessity. The popular prejudice is gradually giving way."

Gradually indeed, for the Sears catalog of 1900 does not list a single gas cooking stove for sale to its customers. Ten years later, a combined gas and coal stove was still considered an innovation. In advertising, husbands were being urged to save their wife time and care by buying her a gas stove.

There can be no question that gas is a cleaner and more efficient cooking fuel than wood or coal. Why then was the gas stove resisted for so long? One reason was that gas once was a more expensive fuel than either coal or wood. But there was a deeper psychological reason. Human beings are extremely conservative about the food that they eat and the way in which it is prepared. Immigrants to a new culture will change their language, the way they dress, even their morals more quickly than they will change their eating habits. People who had grown up with food cooked with wood or coal fuel felt that gas-cooked food somehow "tasted different," or they worried obscurely that the food would not be properly cooked and would therefore be unhealthful. Gas cooking ran squarely into this prejudice.

Ultimately the obvious and overwhelming convenience of the gas stove overwhelmed the old objections, and prejudices and gas cooking moved on to become something of a status symbol. "Now you're cooking with gas," which was an advertising slogan for the gas industry during the 1930s, became a popular phrase that by the 1940s meant "Now you're on the right track."

A notable improvement in the gas stove was the oven regulator, a thermostat that automatically controlled the temperature inside the oven. The regulator was introduced into gas ovens in about 1915 and contributed greatly to their growing popularity. There was no longer a need to check the oven constantly to see if what was inside was being burned or undercooked—the regulator simplified the use of the oven and reduced the number of cooking disasters.

Since the gas stove didn't need a firebox for fuel, the stove could be made smaller. Since the heat sources on the top were reduced in size to a burning ring of gas, part of the top of a stove generally remained cool enough to be used as a working surface. On hot days it was still possible to use a gas stove without turning the kitchen into an inferno. One disadvantage was that on cold days the heat from the cooking stove no longer warmed the entire kitchen. But by the 1920s, most houses that had gas stoves also had central heating, so the extra heat wasn't really necessary anyway.

The earliest gas stoves were made of cast iron and steel, just like the coal and wood stoves they were meant to replace. By the 1930s, all new gas stoves were squared off and covered with white porcelain enamel. As much as anything else this changed the look of the entire kitchen. Now its most prominent and necessary appliance had shrunk to the point where it could be tucked away into a relatively small space, and it was covered with a gleaming, easily cleaned surface.

The next step was the electric stove. It was first

introduced during the 1930s at a time when the gas stove was reaching the height of its popularity. Part of the gas industry's "Now you're cooking with gas" campaign was aimed at the electric stove. The electric stove didn't (and doesn't) look much different from the gas stove. The difference is that the heat source is not an open flame, but a glowing coil. In contrast to the gas stove, which was slow in gaining popularity, the electric stove won quick, if not universal, acceptance.

The electric stove had advantages. It could be heated more quickly. Oven and range-top temperatures could be more delicately controlled and required fewer adjustments. There was no danger of leaking gas. Electric stoves had a "self-cleaning" feature that generally eliminated the need for scrubbing out the oven. The disadvantages were that in the 1930s and 1940s and even later many houses and apartments simply didn't have enough electric current to run an electric stove. The stoves were also more expensive to buy and to operate than the gas stove. With the higher electricity prices of the 1980s, they are proportionally even more expensive to operate.

During the 1970s, microwave cooking was introduced into the American home. This is a very different form of cooking, one that allows for the preparation of certain types of food very, very rapidly. Frozen foods can be cooked in a matter of moments without prethawing. Because it is so different, microwave cooking has met with considerable resistance from the public. Early microwave ovens were considered to be unsafe because they were thought to pose some sort of a radiation hazard. Early microwave ovens did tend to leak radiation, but the danger was exaggerated. The greatest resistance to microwave cooking was rooted

The microwave oven of the 1980s, in combination with an electric stove with a grill. (General Electric)

in the belief that it was somehow unnatural and that the food was not being properly cooked. It was much the same sort of resistance that gas cooking first faced.

The enormous convenience of the microwave oven has helped to break down resistance to its use, particularly in a society where so many people work outside of the home and get back just in time for dinner. Meals that can be prepared in a matter of minutes are highly desirable. But there seems no reason to believe that microwave cooking will replace the gas or electric oven as the primary appliance for food preparation in the home.

A century ago there was the dream of the community kitchen in luxury apartment buildings. As this dream faded, it was replaced by the idea of the efficiency kitchen, a small area in which food could be prepared with great speed. In the years that followed World War II, there were dreams of "push button kitchens" in which all food could be prepared by the push of a few buttons. It was to be the "kitchen of the future."

Prophets of the "kitchen of the future" were very surprised to discover that in the next decade the main move-

A "modern" kitchen of the 1960s shows the renewed popularity of the large kitchen. (Caloric Corporation)

ment was a return to older and more traditional and elaborate methods of cooking. The small efficiency kitchen, the post–World War I dream, was no longer large enough to contain a proliferation of pots, pans, pasta makers, woks, whisks, garlic presses, and all of the other exotic implements necessary for cooking French, Italian, Oriental, or other foods. The truly efficient kitchen even needed a large shelf to contain all of the different kinds of cookbooks that had become so popular.

There was no return to the coal stove, but an echo of this older method of cooking could be found in the rise in popularity of the backyard barbecue. The barbecue, once a regional phenomenon, became nationwide. Every summer weekend, suburban backyards are filled with the smoke produced by meat being burned over charcoal.

While cooking in America has remained primarily the woman's responsibility, during the 1960s it became acceptable for men to do a share of the cooking as well, particularly "gourmet cooking." Many men began to take pride in their ability to cook. The barbecue is an almost exclusively male preserve. Men who still wouldn't be caught dead doing anything in the kitchen will happily don an apron and broil hamburgers or steaks over an outdoor grill.

Cooking is only one part of the process of food preparation. Nearly as important is storing the food. For the home, the big change in food storage that has come over the last century is the development of the refrigerator.

A century ago people kept perishable foods cool in an icebox, which was just that—an insulated box or cabinet with a block of ice inside to keep the air cool. If the box was well insulated, it could keep the air inside cool for several days, depending on how high the outside temperature was and how many times the icebox door had to be opened. But eventually all the ice inside would melt and the water had to be disposed of. New ice had to be purchased. The ice wagon or the ice truck was a familiar sight on city streets. The iceman would take a block of ice out of the wagon or truck with a large pair of tongs, sling the ice over his shoulder (which was covered by a leather pad), and carry it up to the apartment where it was needed. In the summer, kids would follow the ice wagons in order to get slivers of ice to suck on.

In colder weather, people often didn't bother with the icebox. They kept their perishables such as milk on a cold window ledge or in some unheated part of the house.

While it was better than nothing, the icebox was very inconvenient, and food often spoiled. By the 1880s, mechanical methods of refrigeration were already available —indeed much of the ice sold came from icehouses where water was frozen by refrigeration. (In colder climates, it was still cheaper to cut ice from rivers and lakes during the winter and keep it as long as possible into the warmer weather.) Indoor ice rinks where people skated on artificially produced ice were in operation a century ago. The machinery needed to produce the cooling was far too bulky to be used in the home. The problem was not so much one of developing a new technology, but of producing smaller and cheaper versions of what already existed.

The advantages of some sort of mechanical home refrigerator were so obvious that inventors all over the world were working on the problem. Yet progress was extraordinarily slow. It wasn't until the 1920s that home refrigerators became widely available in America, and

America led the world in the use of home refrigeration. Refrigerators were quite expensive at first, so iceboxes were still commonly in use during the 1930s and 1940s. In rural areas where electrification was slow in coming, the icebox held on even longer.

The earliest home refrigerators had dark wood exteriors, just like the icebox's. But they were soon given a streamlined shape and a white porcelain enamel finish so that they fit into the decor of the new kitchen with its white porcelain enamel stove and sink. Early home refrigerators had their disadvantages and their quirks. Food kept for any length of time dried out horribly. Ice built up around the freezing elements, and the refrigerator had to

This 1908 refrigerator and gas range resemble the icebox and wood stove of an earlier era. (New York Public Library Picture Collection)

be defrosted regularly—a messy and time-consuming job. Between defrostings, the ice melted slightly, and it dripped. But with all its faults, the refrigerator represented an enormous advance over what had gone before. And the appliance was constantly being improved. Newer refrigerators contained separate compartments for deep-frozen foods and for foods like milk and eggs that only had to be kept cool. A self-defrosting feature was developed. Gadgets like ice dispensers or iced-tea makers were built directly into the refrigerator. Eventually the relative price of the refrigerator fell to the point where practically everybody could afford one.

The home refrigerator revolutionized shopping. Perishables could be kept for longer periods, so frequent shopping was no longer necessary. Daily home delivery of milk, eggs, and other dairy products was not as necessary as it once had been. In America, the milkman who brought milk to the door every day is now a figure of the past.

Canned goods had been available for well over a century, but the process for quick-freezing food was only patented in 1925. After that the use of frozen foods in the home grew by leaps and bounds. During the 1940s and 1950s, it seemed as though the freezing of foods was going to dominate the preservation of foods, and enormous home freezers became very popular. In these freezers the family was supposed to be able to keep large quantities of meat, frozen vegetables, and other products. But this was one of those innovations that had no real staying power. Some people still have home "deep freezes," buy meat and other products in bulk, and keep them frozen until needed. But most have found that form of shopping inconvenient and have discovered that the savings made by buying in bulk can be wiped out by the energy cost of running a large freezer. For most families, the freezing compartment of the average refrigerator is quite large enough.

Complete frozen dinners that only had to be heated, or TV dinners as they were first called, were another innovation that never lived up to its advance billing. When they were introduced, it seemed as if frozen dinners might be developed into the old utopian dream of meals prepared at a central kitchen. An added advantage was that they required no washing up. After eating the food, you just throw away the foil tray. But while frozen dinners did turn out to be convenient, particularly with microwave ovens, which can heat them in a matter of minutes, they leave a great deal to be desired in the area of taste. And they are expensive for what you get. While frozen dinners are used today, they are now regarded only as a convenience food, and a rather inferior kind at that. Fast-food takeout restaurants have cut deeply into the market for frozen dinners.

Despite all the improvements in cooking and food preservation of the past century, most people would agree that the meal freshly cooked from fresh ingredients is still the best.

Once a meal is over, you have to clean up, and that means washing the dishes—no easy task a century ago in a kitchen that had only a pump and no running hot water at all. Even with running hot and cold water, dishwashing has never been a chore people look forward to. For all its drudgery, cooking has its creative and satisfying side. Dishwashing has no redeeming features—it is sheer drudgery. And that brings us to the automatic dishwasher.

The basic mechanical process behind the modern

dishwasher has been well known for more than a century
—jets of water are sprayed over dishes set in a rack. It wasn't
until about 1915 that the first prototypes of the dishwasher
were put on public display, and it wasn't until the 1930s
that dishwashers were manufactured and offered for sale
to the public. Unlike refrigerators, which came on the
market just a few years earlier, the automatic dishwasher
didn't sweep the nation. Even today the dishwasher is not
considered one of those necessary appliances without which
no kitchen is complete. The simple reason is that the dishwasher really doesn't work very well. Oh, they are a convenience and save some time and effort, but despite what
all the advertising says, they really don't clean pots and
pans with caked-on dirt, nor do they always effectively get
peanut butter off a knife. They don't do the hard washing
jobs. Still they are better than nothing, and most modern
kitchens are provided with a built-in dishwasher.

If there is one thing that our modern age does well
—much too well—it is producing garbage. A century ago,
the owner of a house had to get rid of the ashes from the
furnace and stove. But the volume of ashes was infinitesimal
when compared with the mounds of cartons, cans, bottles,
old newspapers, crumpled junk mail, eggshells, old electric
light bulbs, the litter from the cat's box, and all the rest
of the miscellaneous collection of material that now fills
our garbage cans day after day. We have often been described as a "throwaway" society, a description that is all
too accurate, certainly when compared to past ages.

There have been some attempts to cope with this
enormous mass of garbage in the home; these attempts have
centered in the kitchen. One is the garbage disposal, or
"electric sink," as it once was called. It is essentially a high-

speed shredder attached to the drain on the sink. Garbage is scraped into the shredder and reduced to tiny particles, which are then carried away in the regular sewage pipes by a flow of water.

Garbage disposal is something of a misnomer, for the device rids us of only a small portion of our daily garbage. It takes care of certain types of organic material such as eggshells and potato peels. Metal, paper, plastic, even large bones will jam the machine and render it useless.

The first kitchen sink garbage disposals were available to the public in the early 1930s, but they did not become a standard part of the kitchen until after World War II.

The second device aimed at coping with our throwaway society is the aptly named trash masher or compacter. It is essentially a box with an electrically driven plunger inside. Trash, in this case including the cans, cartons, bottles, and the rest, is simply tossed into a receptacle. The machine is turned on and it squeezes the trash down to a smaller volume. The trash masher, which was yet another of those household gadgets that spread throughout America after World War II, has its disadvantages. If organic garbage is allowed to sit in the device for very long it will rot and smell. Perfumed sprays for trash mashers are sold. Bottles and cans tend to jam the machine. Many owners of trash mashers have given up on them as simply not being worth the trouble.

There is no doubt that the volume of garbage created by our society has created tremendous problems, the most obvious of which is that we are running out of places to put all the garbage. Garbage dumps or landfills are being filled up at an alarming rate. A partial answer to the problem is to stop throwing so much away and to start reusing or recycling as much material as possible. Both the garbage disposal and the trash masher have come under criticism for making the garbage problems worse rather than better.

The garbage disposal turns organic matter into sewage. In so doing it uses up a lot of fresh water at a time when many areas suffer from shortages of fresh water. The sort of garbage that the kitchen sink garbage disposal takes care of can be rotted down and used for garden mulch. This is hardly practical in some cities, but in suburbs, many families have turned off their disposals and started dumping their eggshells and potato peels on a mulch pile in the backyard.

Aluminum, glass, and paper can be recycled at a considerable savings in energy, natural resources, and space in the garbage dump. But in order for recycling to be practical, the various recyclable materials have to be separated out of the mass of trash. The trash masher just squeezes everything together, making separation impossible.

3

The Bathroom

THE TIME HAS come to talk about bathtubs and toilets. Now don't snicker. If you had to wash in cold water on a January morning or use an outdoor privy during a snowstorm, you would soon realize that such subjects are nothing to snicker about.

On the other hand, snickering and what it implies have had a good deal to do with the changes that have and have not taken place in the bathroom over the last century. That's because social attitudes, as much as technology, have shaped this most important room in the house.

Let's take bathing first. The ancient Greeks and Romans thought bodily cleanliness was extremely important. They constructed enormous public baths, which served not only as places to get clean, but also as social centers. Christians deeply distrusted what they considered to be a "pagan" worship of the body, so public bathing, and cleanliness in general, declined after the triumph of Christianity and continued its decline right through the Middle Ages. Some holy men boasted of the fact that they never bathed.

The cities of medieval Europe were notorious for their squalor. But what is less well known is that, in general, standards of personal hygiene continued to fall right through the eighteenth century, the period known as the Enlightenment and the Age of Reason.

Our own enlightened Founding Fathers were probably dirtier in their personal habits than many semi-barbaric castle dwellers of the fifteenth century. Indeed, during the eighteenth century, even the wealthy displayed a supreme indifference to personal filth, preferring to mask odors with the heavy use of perfumes and to cover dirt with makeup. A relationship between dirt and disease was unknown to and unsuspected by them.

The whole world had not given up on bathing. In many parts of the Islamic world, cleanliness was highly prized, and in Turkey the rituals of bathing and personal cleanliness approached fanaticism. The Japanese also valued cleanliness. In the Scandinavian countries and particularly in Russia, steam baths were popular both for getting clean and getting warm. These baths were regularly taken by both sexes together—a practice that shocked many Western travelers.

By the nineteenth century, the idea of regular bathing began to return to Western Europe and to America. Often bathing was presented as a cure for a variety of diseases, rather than for the sake of cleanliness itself and for diease prevention. The Scottish physician John Currie recommended cold-water baths as a treatment for fevers and contagious diseases, while steam baths were said to be good for gout and other ills. It didn't really matter what the reason given was—the idea of taking off one's clothes and getting clean was coming back for the first time in centuries.

Regular bathing, however, was slow to become part of the home, for the simple reason that homes, even wealthy ones, did not have running water. People could wash themselves in a basin. They might even wash their entire bodies, but the water had to be heated, usually in the kitchen, and then carried in buckets to wherever it was the bath was to be taken. After that the tub had to be emptied and the water disposed of somehow. Under such conditions, the bath was a difficult and time-consuming task. One tubful of water was used for several baths.

Most common people in European and American cities were introduced to bathing in public bathhouses. Some bathhouses were set up adjacent to public laundries so they could make use of the surplus hot water. Many public baths were steam baths—usually called Russian, or Turkish, or Oriental baths. The mixed bathing, which had so shocked some travelers to Russia, was not allowed in America. The baths had men's and women's sections, usually served by separate entrances. As a further aid to modesty, some of these Russian or Turkish baths featured private steam cabinets. The bather could climb inside the steam-filled cabinet, with his or her head sticking out. There was no sitting around naked with a lot of other people in a similar state. In addition, one could breathe cool air and a woman's hair would not be disturbed.

An exotic variety of modifications of this personal steam bath were introduced for home use after the middle of the nineteenth century, and they remained popular well into the twentieth century. Though they were cumbersome and impractical in many ways, the reason for the longevity of home steam baths is not difficult to figure out—they required no running water. A small amount of water and a heat source were all that was needed.

Since there was no fixed indoor water supply except perhaps a pump in the kitchen, a tub might be found in any room in the house. A popular item in America around the end of the nineteenth century was the folding tub. The tub was hidden inside a large cabinet or wardrobe and was pulled down for use. The cabinet also contained some sort of water heater that was usually fueled by gas or gasoline. Of course, getting the water to the tub, and especially getting rid of used water afterward, remained major problems. But the folding tub could be placed anywhere in the house and was advertised in the 1895 Montgomery Ward catalog as "a handsome piece of furniture." The potential buyer was also told that the tub was as "perfect in operation as a folding bed." Further, "The cases are of modern designs, excellent quality of cabinet work and thoroughly seasoned hard lumber. The style and finish correspond with the latest and most popular in furniture." The tub itself, a little over five feet long, was made of zinc and had a waste water outlet. The water tank was copper lined. One advantage of this particular folding tub was that it was so well balanced that it didn't have to be attached to the wall.

From the middle of the nineteenth century onward, the shower had generally been regarded as a superior method of washing—it used less water and therefore was more economical. It took less time to shower than to bathe

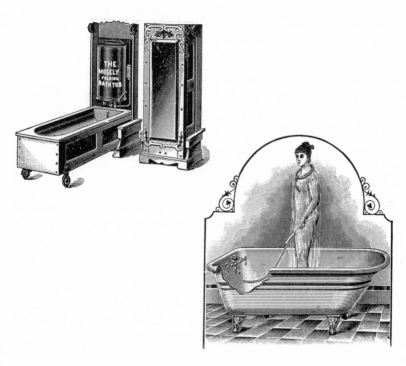

A folding bathtub with built-in water heater sold by Montgomery Ward in 1895. If you had running water, you could order a shower bath ring instead.

and was probably cleaner than the tub bath, because you didn't sit around in dirty water. But for home use the shower had one major disadvantage: it required running water. Therefore during the nineteenth century, showers were used primarily in public bathhouses—where, despite the name, most people took showers instead of baths.

One hundred years ago, most houses did not have a room that could recognizably be called a bathroom. Baths might be taken anywhere in the house or, for city dwellers, outside of the house in a regular bathhouse facility. For most country and city dwellers alike the bath was a rare rather than a regular event, particularly in colder weather.

The second important feature of the modern bathroom is the toilet. A hundred years ago, most homes simply did not have indoor toilets. People depended on one variation or another of the time-honored chamber pot, which was often hidden in an attractive piece of furniture, or they depended on an outhouse or outdoor privy. In some areas, they depended on even more primitive outdoor facilities, or simply on the outdoors. In cities, the disposal of household sewage constituted an enormous problem, and the streets of many cities were described as being "open sewers," a description that a good sense of smell would confirm as being all too accurate. There were many complaints that people who lived in tenements emptied their chamber pots out of convenient windows.

The solution to the disposal of household sewage seems obvious to us: it should be carried away by running water. But why? This is simply a tradition. It is not necessarily based on engineering efficiency or superior sanitation. In his book *Not So Rich As You Think*, George R. Stewart laments the demise of a century-old solution that somehow never caught on—the earth closet. It was invented around 1860 by the Reverend Henry Moule of England and had a lot of devotees by the end of the nineteenth century. Many middle-class private homes in America used the earth closet.

According to Mr. Moule and his many disciples in the later nineteenth century, the earth closet was efficient, wholly inoffensive to have in the house, cheap, simple to work. At least one American company manufactured and distributed it. Stewart writes:

> From a hopper filled with earth, the pulling of a
> lever or even the rising of the person from the seat,

sifted some dry earth into the bowl. All odor was thus contained and the excreta rapidly decomposed and mingled with the earth. They mingled indeed so well that the result could eventually be used again, though this petty economy need not be obligatory.

But note the efficiency in the minimal bulk of product. According to Mr. Moule's published figures, one person needed only two pounds of earth a day. This figure, moreover, was based upon the necessarily crude engineering of a nineteenth century person. What could not our modern experts have developed along this line.

Stewart admits that he views the earth closet as a lost opportunity. "It would certainly have solved some problems. We can imagine the few pounds of earth being picked up with the garbage. Vanished, indeed, would be the flush-toilet, and an army of plumbers would have to be otherwise employed."

But it was not to be. The great drawback was that someone had to clean the earth closet, and once the flush toilet was developed, the earth closet never had a chance. Today most of us would find such a facility in the home almost unthinkable.

Any semblance of the modern bathroom had to await the advent of a system of running water inside the house and a system of sewers to carry away the waste water. In the early part of the nineteenth century, only the wealthiest of homes had anything resembling running water. Most people still relied on water drawn from a lake or river or water pumped from a well in their own front yard or backyard, or from a town pump. Water was carried into the house in a bucket and heated over the stove. Sometimes a pump might be constructed and used inside a kitchen or basement. In some cities, the only source of water for the average household might be a water seller who drove his cart around the neighborhood once or twice a day and sold water by the bucket.

By the middle of the last century, municipal water systems had been established in most of the larger cities of Western Europe and America; development, however, was extremely uneven. Running water was first used extensively in the kitchen and only later for bathing and toilet facilities. Even in cities that had water systems, the running water didn't necessarily run everywhere. At the end of the nineteenth century, New York City had a good municipal water system. But you couldn't tell that to people who lived on the upper floors of tenement buildings because there simply wasn't enough water pressure to push the water beyond the first two or three floors. These tenants still had to go down to street level with a bucket and get their water from the hydrant. The better high-rise buildings had large water tanks on the roofs to supply sufficient water pressure to serve every floor.

In small towns and especially rural areas, running water was still a luxury well into the twentieth century, and among the very poor it is still possible in America to find homes without running water even today.

A modern bathroom doesn't just require water, it requires hot water. First water was heated in the kitchen and carried upstairs or to wherever the bathing or washing was to be done. Then attached to the washbasin, bathtub, or shower came heaters of various designs, which heated the water for that individual facility. Then there were water heaters in the basement that heated the water supply for the entire house, or later, hot water from a central plant that could meet the needs of an entire apartment building.

Less than a hundred years ago, a private bath—that is, one bathroom per family—was a luxury that could be afforded only by the wealthy. Many apartment dwellers counted themselves fortunate if they had access to a bathroom at all, even if it had to be shared with two or three other families. In many cities in America, tenement buildings still relied on a single outdoor privy for twenty or thirty families.

Even when bathing and toilet facilities were brought indoors in tenements, the privacy we now prize was unheard of. Aside from sharing a toilet, families often shared sinks that were in the hall. Reformers who toured tenement buildings in the 1880s were shocked by this. They feared for the morals of children who saw older girls or women washing themselves. Communal bathtubs were sometimes placed in the basement, where there was better water pressure. For moral reasons as much as anything else, builders were encouraged to provide individual bathrooms for each apartment.

In those buildings where apartments had their own toilet and bathing facilities, bathtubs were often found in the kitchen, sometimes placed in a special alcove for the sake of modesty. This placement saved money in construction, for hot-water pipes already ran to the kitchen sink. Cramped tenement dwellers would usually fold down a board over the bathtub when it was not in use, thus turning it into another table, or even a bed at night.

Along with the running water needed for bathing came the running water needed for toilets and the drainage system required to carry away the waste water and sewage.

Compact kitchen of around 1907, complete with bathtub (lower left). (New York Public Library Picture Collection)

In cities, private homes were usually connected to municipal water and sewage systems, whereas in rural areas or smaller towns water might still come from a well—though it was pumped directly into the house, and sewage would drain into a cesspool located under the backyard.

Water and sewage systems have changed remarkably little over the past century. Indeed, in many of America's older cities, systems built a century ago are still in use, although they tend to break down frequently from a hundred years of wear and tear. Still, there has been no absolute need to replace them. Indeed, many of the older systems will outlast systems half their age.

A century ago what bathrooms there were, could be found primarily in wealthy homes and tended to be quite ornate. The fixtures were treated as items of furniture and the 1880s was an era of ornate furniture. The sink, or wash-basin, for example, might be entirely enclosed in a wood-work cabinet with a marble top. As we have seen, the folding tub disappeared into a cabinet, but ordinary tubs, too, could be surrounded by cabinetwork or decorated in a variety of other ways. Even the humble toilet had its touch of "art"—a popular fixture was called "the dolphin." It had a bowl with a shell-like design, supported by a stylized "dolphin" base that concealed the pipes. The whole thing was glazed to an ivory tint. Today the "dolphin toilet" looks almost embarrassingly funny, but in the 1880s and 1890s it was the height of fashion. Bathrooms, particularly in England, tended to be rather large and luxurious, and every attempt was made to hide or disguise their function.

The major problem with all of these luxury adorn-ments, aside from their expense, is that they weren't very practical in a room that was constantly exposed to running water and steam. Wooden cabinets warped and plaster walls crumbled. A new standard for plain but practical bathrooms was developed in America, specifically in Amer-ican hotels, and the hotel influence was soon felt in most homes.

For some reason the idea of having a room with a bath caught on in America much earlier and much more completely than it did in Europe. For many years one of the statistics cited most frequently to prove the superiority of the American way of life was the number of bathtubs in the United States compared to the number of bathtubs elsewhere.

As early as the 1850s, some of the better hotels in the United States were advertising that each room had its own washbasin with hot and cold running water. By the 1880s and 1890s, luxury hotels could offer their guests a private bath—that is, a room with its own separate basin, tub, and toilet. But it wasn't until the first decade of the twentieth century that a room with a private bath became widely available in moderately priced hotels. Fancy fixtures were impractical for moderately priced hotels, so the American type of compact bathroom, with plain and practical fixtures, was developed, and by the 1920s and 1930s, the compact bathroom had become standard in most private homes and apartment buildings. The compact bathroom consisted of sink, tub, and toilet all in white enamel. The tub might have an attached shower, and the tub area could be enclosed by a curtain when the shower was in use. The bathroom floor would be white tile, with the walls either half tiled in white, or simply painted white. All of this was contained in a small room, with an opaque window, and it was conceived of as an appendix to the bedroom. The arrangement was immensely practical if a bit sterile. It endured in America with very little change for decades.

In Europe, the private bathroom was rarer, but larger and more luxurious. According to historian Siegfried Giedion, the European bathroom was treated more as a room with furniture than as a necessary adjunct to the bedroom as it was in America. "England," writes Giedion, "fashioned the luxury bathroom of the world. No other country equaled the quality and distinction of English sanitary articles between 1800 and 1910."

1923 advertisement for "Standard" plumbing fixtures for a five-foot-square bathroom. (New York Public Library Picture Collection)

He describes the English bathroom of about 1900 as a "spacious room possessing a number of windows. The expensive fixtures were placed at dignified distances from one another. The central space was ample enough for moving freely about, even for exercising." But no matter how large the house, there was usually only one bathroom.

Such expansive luxury was rare in America, even in the homes of the very, very rich. The English bathroom could be contrasted with the bathroom of the Fifth Avenue apartment of a member of the Vanderbilt family a century ago. While the Vanderbilt bathroom would certainly have seemed the height of luxury to most Americans at the time (for most had no bathrooms at all), it was still a small room, with the tub, sink, and toilet crowded close together. Even the nickel-plated pipes were left exposed. It was, in short, a highly practical room.

Changes in the typical American bathroom came about slowly and unevenly. A major change was the rise of the shower. While showers had been popular in public bathhouses, most private bathrooms had tubs. Showers, if they existed at all, were appendages to the tub. Since the tub was usually a free-standing object, it had to have a wraparound shower curtain, but that rarely kept the water off the floor. The advent of the recessed tub brought about an improvement in the shower as well. The back part of the tub area could be covered with waterproofed tiles, and only one side had to be protected with a shower curtain— a far less messy arrangement. And as time went on, curtains were sometimes replaced by glass sliding doors, which made the shower practically watertight.

The shower as a separate unit was not ordinarily part of the American bathroom during the early years of the twentieth century. The separate shower was associated with the public bathhouse, and on those rare occasions when it was used in a private home, the shower stall tended to be a dreary zinc-lined affair, which carried with it a vivid reminder of its public bathhouse origins. Gradually the idea of a home shower grew in popularity, and in the American housing boom that followed World War II, many new homes and apartments were equipped with separate tiled shower stalls, which had sliding glass doors. As the shower replaced the tub bath as the favored means of bathing at home, a bathroom with its own shower stall became a valued addition to any home.

At about the same time, the austere, functional, all-white, compact bathroom that had been the standard in America for decades began to change. Color was added in fixtures, in wall tiles, and in floor coverings. The bathroom took over more functions. At one time men would shave in their bedrooms, using the mirror over the dresser and water in a basin. Or as often as not, they were shaved outside the home in barbershops. But as the twentieth century wore on, shaving became an activity performed almost exclusively in the bathroom. The same progression from bedroom to bathroom took place with makeup. One hundred years ago, women had dressing tables in their bedrooms or in small dressing rooms near the bedroom. That was where makeup was kept and applied. As this activity too was transferred more and more to the bathroom, the room that had once been dimly lit acquired powerful lighting and larger mirrors.

Most bathrooms in the early years of this century didn't have medicine cabinets. People kept their medicines in cabinets in other rooms of the house—usually in the bedroom. But the bathroom medicine cabinet, which was practically universal by the 1940s, became the repository of all household medicines, not to mention a variety of hair-, skin-, and teeth-care items.

Electricity has become an increasingly important part of the modern bathroom. If you happen to find yourself in a bathroom that has not been renovated since 1940 or even 1950, see if you can find a convenient place to plug in your hair dryer or electric razor. There may be an outlet in the baseboard far away from the mirror or there may be no outlet at all. In the 1940s and 1950s, there were no hand-held hair dryers (although some people did use vacuum cleaners for that purpose). Electric razors were still rare. Men often bought them so that they could shave in the bedroom again and thus wouldn't have to shave in the home's single crowded bathroom. There were no electric curling irons, no makeup mirrors with special lights, no electric heaters for shaving lather, and no electric toothbrushes for cleaning your own teeth or ultrasonic devices for cleaning false teeth. The bathroom didn't have electric outlets because it didn't need them. But like most other rooms in the house, the use of electricity in the bathroom has increased enormously. Nevertheless, many of the electric bathroom gadgets are now battery operated.

In the late nineteenth century, bathing was regarded as a health-promoting activity, rather than a mere cleaning one. In modern times, there has been something of a return to that idea, with the introduction of devices that turn an ordinary tub bath into a whirlpool bath meant to promote muscle relaxation and general good health. Heat lamps and sun lamps are sometimes part of a modern bathroom.

A bath with whirlpool is sometimes a feature of modern, more luxurious bathrooms. It represents yet another step away from the functional, yet austere, compact bathroom. (Jacuzzi Whirlpool Bath)

With all the new functions that bathrooms have acquired in recent years, it is not surprising to discover that they have become both larger and more numerous. The house or large apartment with a single bathroom is a rarity. Still, one of the most common complaints heard in most households is that someone else is "hogging the bathroom."

Bathing or showers that were once a weekly ritual at best are now a daily and in some cases twice daily activity. Hot-water systems have been expanded to try to cope with the growing demand, but somebody usually winds up with a cold shower anyway.

For those who can afford it, the bathroom can become a truly luxurious part of the house with inlaid tile floors, faucets that look like swans, and sunken tubs that resemble swimming pools more than they do the old-fashioned bathtub. There has, as yet, been no return to the "dolphin toilet," or anything like it, but such a development is not inconceivable.

A couple of bathing innovations imported from abroad are so large that they don't properly fit in the bathroom. One is the sauna—an adaptation of the steam baths that were once popular. But the sauna was reintroduced from Scandinavia, not as a public bath or cabinet, but as a small wood enclosed room, heated electrically. It is supposed to promote not only cleanliness, but general health as well. An adaptation of the Japanese hot tub has also become popular, but in the United States it is used less for cleaning or warming, its primary function in Japan, than to promote the healthful social attitudes that are supposed to flow from mixed nude bathing. It remains a highly controversial innovation.

Yet, in many respects the bathroom has changed less than other parts of the house. The basic ingredients of sink, tub, and toilet have remained the same since running water was first introduced into the home. Most of us would find a kitchen from around the turn of the century almost impossible to cook in. Yet a well-maintained bathroom from the same era would be perfectly serviceable.

4

Keeping Warm, Keeping Cool

IF SOMEONE WHO had lived one hundred years ago were by some miracle set down in a house today, the only "new" item he or she might recognize instantly is the recently installed wood-burning stove.

There is a great deal of irony in the modern return to older forms of heating, and we will look at this return more carefully a little later. First, let's see what things were like a century ago.

While central heating was far from universal in the 1880s, the better and more modern middle-class homes were usually heated by a coal-fired furnace in the cellar. The heated air from the furnace would be forced into large ducts and would enter a room through a grate or register in the floor. The heat delivered by such a system was generally very dry. When the heat was on, there was always a draft of hot air issuing from the register. In a large room, one part might be very warm, while at a distance from the register the air might still be uncomfortably cool.

The hot-water system, which became increasingly popular around the turn of the century, was considered to be more efficient and heated the rooms more evenly. In this system, hot water heated by the furnace was circulated through pipes and into metal radiators in each room. The radiators warmed the air around them and thus warmed the room. When the system wasn't working quite properly, radiators and pipes banged and rattled abominably. But in general, hot-water heating worked fairly well. As with the heated air from the coal-fired furnace, the heated air from hot-water heating was extremely dry. People would try to counteract the dryness—particularly when someone in the house had a cold—with pans placed on top of or hung behind the radiators. Some moisture was put back into the air by evaporation from the pans, but in truth the pans didn't help very much. Dry air was a small price to pay for keeping warm.

The radiator itself presented something of an interior decorating problem, for it could be a large and rather ugly fixed object. Sometimes radiators were hidden in cabinets or disguised with some sort of ornate radiator cover. Unfortunately the more efficiently the radiator was hidden, the less efficiently it delivered heat.

As was mentioned, central heating in the 1880s was far from universal. In small towns and rural areas as well as in many city homes and apartment buildings, the principal source of heat was still a room stove. Merchants and mail-order houses offered an incredible variety of stoves that heated with wood, coal, oil, or gas. Some of these

Bringing home the oldest form of fuel, wood, about one hundred years ago. (New York Public Library Picture Collection)

stoves would double as cooking stoves or as water heaters for washing. There were also specialty stoves, for example, a laundry stove designed primarily for heating water for washing laundry or for boiling certain kinds of laundry such as the baby's diapers. When the room stove was replaced by central heating, as it was almost universally in America by the 1950s, it was thought that the stove would never come back. That only goes to show that even the safest-seeming predictions can sometimes be very wrong.

The stove of one sort or another had been the preferred form of room heating for well over a century before the 1880s. Remember that one of the Founding Fathers of the United States, Benjamin Franklin, had made important improvements in the stove during the 1750s. In fact, the Franklin stove, though modified, was still in use during the late nineteenth century.

The middle-class house and the apartment of a century ago often contained one or more fireplaces. Even in homes built with central heating the fireplace remained. In such homes, there was no good practical reason for having a fireplace and there hadn't been for a long time. For many years, the fireplace had been recognized as a thoroughly inefficient way of heating a room. But the fireplace wasn't being used only for its heat-producing qualities. Even a century ago, the fireplace had become a symbol of an earlier and presumably better era of domestic life. The family seated around the fireplace on a winter evening or the man of the house seated in his easy chair in front of the fireplace with his faithful dog at his feet are enduring images in America. Never mind that the roaring fire bakes one side of a person, while the other is allowed to freeze, or that the fireplace is often being used in an already centrally heated room. It's the image that counts.

Writes Gwendolyn Wright in *Building the Dream,*

> One popular symbol of domesticity was the fireplace. By the 1870s, although furnaces or room stoves

had taken over the task of heating most suburban homes, fireplaces had become popular symbols of the family hearth. Elaborately carved mantels, some in marble but most in inexpensive painted and incised wood, provided the suburban home with its ritual center. It did not matter if some hearths were fitted with imitation logs, fired by gas, or hid a furnace register.

Even centrally heated apartments were often provided with fireplaces in order to give them a more homey look. The majority of these apartment fireplaces had never been anything but decorations. Indeed, it would have been quite impossible to put working fireplaces in large apartment buildings because there would be no space for all the necessary chimneys.

During the 1920s and 1930s, the popularity of fireplaces, particularly the artificial ones, declined; many were bricked up or closed off with ornamental metal plates. Later occupants who were once again attracted to the idea of having a wood-burning fireplace in the living room would often open these long-closed fixtures, only to be disappointed to discover that all they had was an ornamental hole in the wall.

The popularity of fireplaces rose after World War II —but not ornamental fireplaces with gas or electric logs. Only real fireplaces that burned wood (or some sort of chemical log that looked like wood) were wanted. By that time, fireplaces were extremely expensive to build and quite wasteful to operate. In addition to being a symbol of domesticity, they had become a status symbol. The symbol is still with us very powerfully today. When you watch television, notice how often a fireplace appears in the background of ads. There are the happy family at Christmas-time, the glamorous young couple sharing a glass of wine, or the obviously wealthy and successful man in his study. And so often in the background there is the roaring fire in the fireplace.

Fireplaces aside, it wasn't wood that was keeping Americans or, for that matter, the citizens of most of the industrialized nations of the world warm during the last hundred years. Early in this century, the major fuel was coal, used in coal-fired furnaces or coal stoves. The coal delivery truck was a familiar sight on the streets of most cities during the first half of the twentieth century. Some-times the coal would simply be dumped in a huge pile outside of an apartment building and then shoveled into the basement through a window. A better method was the coal chute, which allowed the coal to be poured directly into the basement from the dump truck. Small quantities of coal for room stoves could be purchased and brought home in baskets. Homes with coal stoves would store coal in the cellar; the coal would then be carried up in pails or coal scuttles when needed.

Coal not only fueled homes, it fueled much of the world's industry as well. Coal was efficient, abundant, and relatively cheap. But it had its drawbacks—coal was bulky, which made it hard to transport, and it was dirty when you burned it. In industrial areas, trees, houses, streets, and, as it turned out, people's lungs became coated with the by-products of burning coal. Thickly settled residential areas were subjected to smog, a mixture of pollutants from many different sources including coal smoke. It was a long time before the public recognized the dangers of such pollutants. It took disasters like the London killer fog of December

Automatic coal stoker of the 1940s. Coal was put into the hopper (left), and when the temperature fell below a preset level, coal was automatically transferred from the hopper to the furnace (right). Such a device was more practical for apartment buildings than private homes. (New York Public Library Picture Collection)

1952, which was responsible for some 5,000 deaths and as many as 100,000 cases of serious illness, to finally awaken people to the dangers. Much of the London smog was caused by the use of coal stoves, which heated the homes of most Londoners. Something had to be done about coal, and fortunately another cleaner fuel was at hand—oil.

Oil, too, was a polluting fuel, but it was not nearly so bad as coal. Owing to major oil discoveries first in the United States and then in the Middle East, oil was plentiful and cheap. Oil in the form of gasoline powered the American automobile industry. And oil, along with natural gas, became the fuel of choice for heating homes. In many urban areas, the use of coal was banned entirely as being too dirty. Homeowners rushed to change from coal-fired furnaces to oil and gas furnaces. Aside from being cleaner, oil and gas heat were a lot more convenient. There was no need for a large coal cellar in a house. The furnace did not have to be fed; that is, coal didn't have to be shoveled into it at regular intervals. One of the most disagreeable tasks for a homeowner a hundred years ago was the winter morning trip to the cellar to stoke the furnace. During the night, the coal fire in the furnace was allowed to burn low and the temperature of the house dropped. First thing in the morning, somebody had to go down into the basement and put more coal into the furnace so that it would burn hotter and warm the house. That was a dirty job no one wanted. With oil or gas heat that could all be eliminated. There was no need to feed the fire; it was done automatically. A properly working gas or oil furnace didn't have to be touched during a heating season. The temperature of the house could be raised or lowered by the twist of a thermostat.

As far as home heating in America was concerned, the years between 1950 and the early 1970s represented a Golden Age of sorts. Fuel was cheap. Then in 1973 the Middle Eastern countries, which had come to control the lion's share of the world oil market, realized just what a valuable commodity they had and how dependent the industrialized world had become on their oil. They turned off the oil faucet, and they wouldn't turn it on again until they received fourfold, fivefold, or tenfold what they had been getting previously for their oil. That produced an economic shock that resulted in major changes in the way we live. In the early 1980s, the stranglehold of Middle

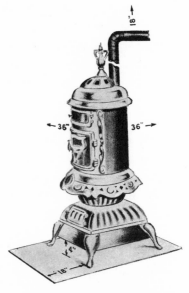

COAL STOVE—CIRCULATING TYPE

COAL STOVE—RADIATING TYPE

GAS STOVE—CIRCULATING TYPE

GAS-STEAM AND GAS-HOT WATER RADIATORS

Three types of stoves and the radiator that were commonly used for heating during the first half of the twentieth century. (New York Public Library Picture Collection)

Eastern oil sheikhs was not as tight as it had been, and oil prices had even dropped a bit. But most experts agreed that such a situation was a temporary one. In any case, the idea that oil and natural gas were cheap and abundant fuels that could be used almost indiscriminately had evaporated forever. Even if the price of oil had not been raised so dramatically, it would have risen steadily anyway, for oil is a nonrenewable resource. As the easy sources of oil are being used up, it becomes more difficult (and expensive) to produce. The same is true for natural gas.

During the 1950s and the 1960s, many persons bought "all electric" homes. These are houses in which the heating as well as the appliances are electric. All-electric homes were cleaner, they seemed more efficient, and heating with electricity was not much more expensive than heating with oil—at the time. But, as people discovered after 1973, electricty was not just something that came out of a socket. Electric power had to be generated somewhere, usually in plants that were fueled by oil. When the price of oil went up, the cost of electric heating went up even more. The oil-fired furnace in the home makes more efficient use of fuel for producing heat than does the distant electric generating plant. In many parts of the country, electric heat was priced right out of the market. Many people who had been sold all-electric homes just a few years earlier were no longer able to afford maintaining or owning such homes; they were understandably bitter.

A return to coal has been proposed—but the old problem of pollution remains. Besides, the facilities for both production and transportation of coal deteriorated during the years of oil supremacy, and rebuilding the system would be enormously costly. More coal will be used in the future, but it's impossible to predict how much more.

The glowing promise of nuclear energy has not been fulfilled. After World War II, some advocates of nuclear power said that nuclear power would make electricity so abundant and cheap that cost would barely have to be considered. As it has turned out, nuclear generating plants are far, far more expensive and difficult to operate than the early proponents of nuclear energy had foreseen. Even though rigid safeguards are built into the plants (that being one of the reasons they are expensive to operate), the majority of Americans still don't trust them. There are plenty of experts who insist that at the present stage of technology nuclear generating plants are not really safe. The 1979 near disaster in the nuclear generating plant at Three Mile Island shocked everyone. Another such near disaster might actually bring the age of nuclear power to an abrupt end in the United States.

The problem of disposing of nuclear wastes has never been solved in a satisfactory manner. Nuclear power is now regarded with a great deal of apprehension, and its future is still in doubt. Even some defenders of nuclear power are beginning to speak of it as a stopgap measure, not a final solution to energy problems. It is something to be used until better solutions come along.

Solar power is being touted as the true energy source of the future. Some homes and apartment buildings are now heated or partially heated by the energy collected in solar panels. But the use of this sort of energy is still in the experimental stage, and it is not yet a major heating source for homes.

The old-fashioned windmill has been resurrected and

Kurt Wasser, publisher of *Solar Age,* shows a simple and inexpensive type of solar energy collector that he has invented.

modernized as a way of providing energy. But windpower, too, is still very much in the experimental stage.

People have responded to the rise in fuel prices primarily by trying to use less of it. On the average, homes in the United States are colder during the winter in the 1980s than they were during the 1960s. Europeans, and the British in particular, have always regarded the Americans as shamefully wasteful of heat. English visitors to America would often complain of what they considered the stifling temperatures at which Americans kept their homes during the winter—75° or 80°F—even at night.

On the other hand, American visitors to England would grumble and shiver in rooms that were as low as 55°F.

Now the Americans are getting used to being more like the British. Temperatures are lower. People wear sweaters in the house. Long underwear, once the subject for jokes, has again become a popular item of winter wearing apparel, even inside the house. It is no longer common in the northern part of the United States to find people wearing short sleeves inside the house during the winter.

In this new energy-conscious environment, the room stove has made a comeback. In areas where wood is plentiful, people have found that a wood stove makes an excellent supplementary source of heating. Stove technology has improved over the last century so that today it has become a more efficient form of heating. Once-decorative fireplaces have been filled with one or another type of stove. Homeowners may miss the sight of a roaring fire, but the stove helps cut down on fuel bills. Even where fireplaces are left intact they have been fitted out with blowers or other devices to improve their efficiency as heating units. Of course, where wood is expensive the wood-burning stove is no bargain. Where such stoves are used extensively, they do create air pollution problems.

Coal stoves have come back into favor in some areas, and so have kerosene and electric heaters. As with the wood stove, these are usually supplements to a central heating system. While electric heating is, as we mentioned, expensive, it is far more economical to heat a single room or a portion of a room that is used frequently, than to turn up the thermostat and raise the temperature of the entire house. So an electric spot heater comes in handy.

During the mid-1970s and early 1980s as fuel prices

skyrocketed, there was a virtual orgy of insulating and sealing of homes. In the days of low-priced oil, there seemed little need to go through the trouble of adding extra insulation or making sure that every door and window was properly draft free. Before 1973, all one had to do was turn up the heat a bit—it didn't cost much.

The rising cost of energy has affected the way that homes in America are built. The enormous picture windows and sliding glass patio doors that were once the pride of the suburban homeowner are no longer as popular as they once were. Such vast expanses of glass radiate a great deal of heat. In the winter, such doors and windows are covered with thick insulating drapes. Rooms with extremely high ceilings are also expensive and difficult to heat, and so there are fewer of them being built. Smaller more easily heated rooms are now favored.

A century ago, people worried about getting enough fuel to keep their homes warm in the winter. Then, for a while, with cheap oil, that concern seemed to evaporate for most Americans. They could afford to keep their houses as warm as they liked. That trend has been reversed; most Americans have been forced to rediscover the energy-frugal ways of their ancestors.

Keeping warm in a cold climate has been a problem for the human race since the days of cave people. Keeping cool has never been as pressing a problem—you can freeze to death more easily than you can die from overheating. But while heat and humidity didn't usually kill people who lived in temperate climates, it could make them awfully uncomfortable. One hundred years ago people escaped the heat as best they could. The lucky ones (usually those with money) got away during the hottest months to the cooler mountains, lakes, or the seashore. Children would go swimming in any available body of water, while adults fanned themselves and just tried to move more slowly. People would sit around on the front porch—if they had one— to catch the breeze—if there was one. The screened-in porch appeared around the turn of the century, with the mass production of wire mesh. Tenement dwellers would lean

Keeping cool in the slums. (New York Public Library Picture Collection)

out of windows or sit and even sleep on fire escapes—anything to find relief from the airless heat inside the cramped apartments.

The morals of the time made keeping cool more difficult than it had to be. What is considered comfortable summer clothing today would have been regarded as highly immodest a century ago: a woman seen on the street in a halter top and shorts would have been arrested immediately. People had to keep covered up no matter how hot they felt. Even the fabrics were heavier than they are today.

A century ago the only widely available device that could provide any relief from the heat was the hand fan. You waved it to and fro in front of your face, and it created a current of air that evaporated the perspiration and thus cooled you—a little bit anyway. There were mechanical devices that allowed fans to be operated by a lever and cord. This could be attached to a pedal. Thus you didn't have to wave your hand to create a breeze; you had to move your foot. One inventor came up with a fan operated by a rocking chair. As you rocked back and forth, you pulled a cord that moved the fan attached to the ceiling. Several varieties of fans run by clockwork were also built, but these were not very powerful. For the amount of cooling they supplied (which was very little), they were not considered to be worth the price.

It was the genius Nikola Tesla who developed the electric fan in 1889. The fan was the first practical use for Tesla's newly patented small electric motor. The little electrically driven three-bladed fan represented an enormous improvement over any previous form of mechanical cooling. But there was a problem: in order to use it, you

An electric fan of 1894. (New York Public Library Picture Collection)

needed an electric current and in 1889 electrical transmission was still in its infancy. The first large-scale electrical generating plant wasn't even built until 1896, and for many years afterward, there was still a lively argument as to whether electricity would ever be inexpensive enough to be used in the average home.

But as electric transmission systems began to spread in the early years of the twentieth century, the electric fan was already there waiting to be used. And used it was. In many homes it was the first electrical appliance to be purchased. There have been all manner of variations, ceiling fans, rotating fans, window fans, variable speed fans, and so forth, but they are all basically identical to Tesla's original model, and they all share the same drawback— they move the air, but they don't cool it.

The next step in providing cooling for the home was to actually lower the temperature of the air, the process that we now call air conditioning. Modern air conditioning is the end product of a long and complex development that began in the 1840s. Air conditioning was first used in textile mills, not as a means of keeping the workers cool, but in order to help regulate the moisture content of the textiles. Air conditioning wasn't used for human comfort until 1922 when it was installed as an experiment in a motion picture theater. The experiment was a fantastic success. Soon air conditioning was as great a summer attraction in the theaters as the movies themselves, and when the air conditioning broke down—as it often did—patrons angrily demanded their money back. From 1925 until 1955, "Relax in Air Conditioned Comfort" was the siren call of the movie palace on a hot July night.

The use of air conditioning soon spread to other public buildings such as restaurants and department stores. During the 1930s, small self-contained air-conditioning units were developed, and while they were first used in railroad cars, they were easily adapted for use in the home.

But the development of the practical home air conditioner was interrupted by the war. After World War II, there was an explosion in the use of home air conditioning. New homes were often built with central air conditioning or with built-in air-conditioning units. All but the most cheaply built of new apartment buildings were air conditioned, and small window units were available for older homes and apartments.

While air conditioning was a convenience and a comfort for the northern part of the United States, it was a revolutionary development for much of the South. Cities like Miami and Houston, which had been intolerable in the summer months, could now be made bearable, even comfortable. As the use of air conditioning spread to practically every facet of daily life, it became possible for an individual to spend nearly all of his or her time in an air-conditioned environment—just as it had long been possible in a cold climate to spend almost all of one's time in a heated environment. This tremendous change took place in less than thirty years and contributed a great deal to the growth and prosperity of many areas in the South. Without air conditioning, most people would find Houston so hot and humid as to be unlivable. With air conditioning, it is the fastest-growing city in the country. Air conditioning isn't the only reason for the growth, but it is a major contributor.

The air conditioner is a great consumer of electricity. Back in the 1950s when most people in America lugged home their first air conditioner (a bulky noisy monster), they found that they had to have their homes rewired in order to use it properly. If they didn't provide a separate line for the energy-gulping air conditioner, every time they turned it on they would blow a fuse. Even in a rewired house, the lights would flicker ominously when the air conditioner was switched on, and if people were foolish enough to try and use some other high-energy-consuming appliance—the electric iron, for example—while the air conditioning was running, they would still blow a fuse. Homeowners had to check to see that every other appliance in the house was off before venturing to turn on the air conditioner.

The greatest drains on the electric power in cities come during the summer months, primarily because of the use of air conditioners. Many of the major blackouts and power shortages that have hit urban areas can be traced directly to the increased power demand created by the use of air conditioning. In New York City the peak time for electrical use comes at five or six o'clock on a hot summer day when people get home from work and switch on the air conditioner.

When the price of electric power jumped, the air conditioner suddenly became a very, very expensive item indeed because it uses a lot of electric power. This forced a change both in technology and living habits.

Air-conditioning units were made more energy efficient. Once buyers had only been interested in how fast an air conditioner could cool a room. Now they wanted to know how much that convenience would cost them. The superiority of central air conditioning for the home was questioned. Why cool the whole house when all you really needed was a cool bedroom? The average summer temperature in air-conditioned homes (as well as in theaters, department stores, and other public places) rose. It was considered sufficient just to be cooler—you didn't have to be cold. Sitting around an air-conditioned room in a sweater is just as wasteful as sitting around a heated room in a short-sleeved shirt.

The economical electric fan made a comeback. It was discovered that an exhaust fan in an attic window was a fairly efficient way of lowering the air temperature of a house at night. Hot air was pulled out of the house and cool air in. The system worked with nature, it didn't try to overpower nature. Even a large fan is cheap to operate when compared to an air conditioner. A ceiling fan used in conjunction with an air conditioner keeps a room cooler at less cost by moving the heavier cold air around.

The air conditioner has become a permanent part of the American home. It is not going to disappear no matter how expensive it is to operate. As with heating, people have simply become more conscious of the cost of air conditioning. We are forced to pause and think for a moment before switching it on, and we are now looking for ways to keep from switching it on so often or turning it up so high.

5

Light
and
Power

THE LATE NINETEENTH century has often been called the gaslight era. That name has a nice romantic flavor to it, creating an image of rooms bathed in the soft, flickering, yellowish glow of the gaslight.

As with most labels, "the gaslight era" is somewhat misleading. Coal gas had been used for illumination since the early years of the nineteenth century. Gaslighting was first introduced in London around 1815, and by mid-century, gas for light was available to virtually the entire city and to many other cities in the British Isles as well. Gaslighting was demonstrated in the United States as early as 1796. In 1816 Baltimore, Maryland, became the first American city to install a system of gas pipes for city lighting. The gaslight industry continued to grow until nearly the end of the nineteenth century.

The gas for lighting was manufactured at a central

point, an unpleasant and smelly establishment called the gashouse or gasworks, usually located in the poorest part of town. Gas was then carried by pipes to the places where it was used. Of course, that meant that gas was only available in cities, for it was unprofitable and perhaps technically impossible to run gas pipes over long distances. Small towns and certainly rural areas had no facilities for the manufacture and delivery of gas. There never was a gaslight era on the farm.

Even where illuminating gas was available, it had its dangers and drawbacks. Gas burned with an open flame, and thus there was the ever-present danger of fires. It produced noxious fumes, which were "so unpleasant," wrote one observer, "that in the new Madison Square theater every gas jet is ventilated by small tubes to carry away the products of combustion." Gas was more useful for outdoor lighting, such as streetlights, or for illuminating large public rooms, theaters, restaurants, and the like, than it was for lighting the smaller rooms of private homes. While the homes of wealthy and middle-class city dwellers one hundred years ago often did possess gaslights, at least in the living room, gas was too expensive for the poor. Besides, one hundred years ago three-quarters of all Americans lived in small towns and rural areas where there was no gas. The great advantage of gaslight was that it could be turned on and off with ease. There was no lamp to be filled, no wick to be trimmed.

One hundred years ago, most people lighted the insides of their homes, as they had for centuries before, with kerosene or oil lamps and candles. Even in gaslit homes, bedrooms and halls required a candle or lamp. Lamps had to be filled, lighted, and carefully tended. Yet lamps would still blow out at inappropriate moments. They produced unpleasant fumes, and as with all open flames, there was the danger of fire. Candles were expensive, and they blew out even more frequently. Neither lamps nor candles, nor gaslights for that matter, were particularly efficient producers of light. One hundred years ago, people spent much more of their time in darkness or semidarkness than we do today. Romantic perhaps, but it made reading at night difficult. Those romantically gaslit streets were also the haunts of criminals who hid easily in the all too abundant shadows.

A new and better source of illumination was clearly needed, and it was obvious to the technically minded of

Lamps sold by Montgomery Ward & Company in 1895.

the nineteenth century that the power for this new light would be electricity. The problem of electric light was worked on by scientists and inventors throughout the nineteenth century. In 1808, Sir Humphry Davy had demonstrated that a bright light could be produced in a gap between two carbon rods when a strong electric current was passed through them. This form of lighting was called arc lighting, for the light that filled the gap took the form of an arc.

Arc lighting seemed promising, but it also presented a host of problems primarily because it required a strong and reliable source of electric current. As the methods of generating electricity slowly improved, practical uses were made of arc lighting. Outdoor arc lighting had been displayed with spectacular success at the Paris Exposition of 1878. It was said to be the finest artificial light ever seen. Yet the lights shown in Paris were not practical for home use, and a virtual army of inventors was hard at work trying to improve the electric light. Fame and a great deal of fortune awaited the developer of a practical electric light.

Oddly, the man who is generally credited with being the real inventor of the electric light—Thomas A. Edison—entered the field rather late. Like every other inventor, he had tinkered with the idea but at first did no serious work. In 1877, Edison had demonstrated his first prototype of the phonograph, and it wasn't until the following year that he entered the electric light sweepstakes in earnest.

Edison rarely did anything by half measures. In the fall of 1978, he began making public pronouncements about electric lights. He told a reporter that he should have a practical electric light ready for demonstration in about six weeks. When he made that statement he had not even started work. This was the first of a long series of overly optimistic predictions that Edison made about the speed with which he could solve the problems of electric lighting.

It wasn't just that Edison had supreme confidence in his abilities to solve the practical problems of lighting quickly. More significantly, he had people who had invested money in his work to be kept quiet and satisfied and he needed more money and investors. So Edison had to keep promising great things and great profits for the very near future to keep his nervous investors happy and to attract new investors.

Oddly, for a man who was as practical minded as Edison, he was often a careless businessman. Edison was chronically short of cash, and never more so than in 1878. He tried to overcome this problem in his usual way, by lulling investors into a false sense of security by making impossible promises, and then driving himself and his associates day and night in order to fulfill the promises. It took Edison many times six weeks to develop an electric light, but history has forgotten that. For even if he did miss his deadline, he developed the light.

What separated Edison from most of the others working on the electric light was the type of light he wanted to create. Most inventors were working on some sort of improvement or modification of the arc light. But Edison believed that this sort of lighting had no real future, for it was far too bright and required too much power to ever be practical in the home. Edison decided that the home was the place where the electric light would be most important.

In the same interview in which he gave himself a six-week deadline, Edison outlined his plans for the future of electric lighting. From a central station there would be a network of wires that would reach into every home and deliver the current to run small household lights. In some way (as yet unknown), the usage of electric light would be measured—metered as we would now say—and paid for. That is precisely what came to pass.

Before that goal was reached, Edison faced the problem of constructing a practical electric light. Edison believed the future lay in the production of an incandescent light. It was well known that when an electric current was passed through a thin filament of certain materials it would cause those materials to become incandescent—to glow. Experiments with this sort of lighting had been going on in a rather desultory way since about 1820. So little progress had been achieved that to many the incandescent light seemed like a dead end. Edison, however, saw in the incandescent light a softer glow, produced with less electric power. It was the kind of light that could be used in the home.

The invention of the electric light—what we now call the light bulb—did not come as the result of any single master stroke. There was no "Eureka moment" or sudden solution to *the key* problem. Rather it was the result of tediously overcoming innumerable but related practical problems. For example, incandescent substances tended to break down and thus become useless after only a brief exposure to the air. It was known that if the substance was made to glow within a vacuum, it would continue to glow much, much longer. Other inventors had worked on this principle for years without ever producing a practical light.

Thomas Edison at work in 1905. (Con Edison)

Most had given up on the approach as impossible. But Edison took it up, and by a long series of trial and error experiments he was able to produce a reliable vacuum within a thin glass container or bulb. That meant he needed bulbs of the proper thickness, and producing them presented a flock of new problems that had to be solved. Edison and his associates virtually had to design a new electric generating system to provide power for the light.

Probably the most difficult problem that Edison faced was finding material that could be made to glow inside the bulb. The closest thing to a major breakthrough Edison achieved in his experiments was the discovery that a carbonized thread made a superior element for the light. This breakthrough came only after frustrating months of testing and retesting one sort of material after the other. One of the main differences between Edison and his less successful contemporaries was that he never gave up.

All the while the testing was going on Edison kept making optimistic and unrealistic predictions about his imminent success, even though his original six-week deadline had long passed, and others working on the electric light problem seemed to be on the verge of their own breakthroughs. There was a race going on, and Edison often said that his main spur was his desire to finish ahead of the other inventors.

To keep his investors and the press happy, Edison kept giving public demonstrations of his "success" even when he wasn't very successful. Sometimes the demonstrations seemed successful only because of a little trickery. Edison would quickly turn off the glowing bulb just before he knew it was about to fizzle out.

Other times the demonstrations were unqualified disasters. Edison biographer Robert Conot describes what happened on March 22, 1889, at a demonstration held in Edison's Menlo Park, New Jersey, laboratory:

> The gaslights were turned off. Edison ordered the resistance boxes cut out one by one. As the current increased, the sixteen lamps mounted above the workmen's benches glowed red . . . yellow . . . white. Each lamp produced 22 candlepower—compared to the 16 candlepower obtained from a gas jet—and the visitors exclaimed with pleasure as the machines were etched sharply like three-dimensional drawings on white paper.
>
> Within a few seconds, however, the lights commenced flickering. Sparks shot from the contact points

of one lamp, then another, as the circuit was opened by the thermal regulators. The flashing increased whenever the current was interrupted on two lamps simultaneously. The stockholders, taken aback, flinched and shielded their eyes.

Suddenly, one light grew in intensity. A sharp crack resounded through the room. The glass shattered. A row of lamps died out. . . . After a minute or two, another globe burst. One by one the number of lamps was reduced. Soon the visitors had seen enough.

On a later occasion, Edison was to demonstrate the use of electric light in his own home. But as he prepared for the demonstration, one of the globes burst and set fire to his parlor carpet. As the visitors arrived, Mrs. Edison tactfully informed them that they would not be able to go to the parlor because it was being "remodeled."

Officials of the highly profitable illuminating gas industry did all they could to discredit Edison's work in the press.

In the end, Edison triumphed. By December 1880, he had unquestionably produced a workable electric light system. He gave a huge demonstration at his laboratory, and this time nothing went wrong.

The next step was to evolve an electrical transmission system so that electricity could be brought into every home. Here, too, Edison was a leader and a prophet. He had already repeatedly declared his faith in electricity as the power source of the future. If the nineteenth century belonged to steam power, said Edison, then the twentieth century would surely be the century of electricity. One hundred years ago that sounded to many like a wild prediction, but it was absolutely correct.

In 1880 and 1881, Edison moved some of his operation to New York City, and he began installing electric lights along Fifth Avenue. These attracted a great deal of attention and soon there was a demand by wealthy individuals to have their homes electrified. One millionaire had electric lights installed on his yacht.

The decades of the 1880s and 1890s saw great improvements in the generation and transmission of electricity. By the early twentieth century, electric lights had almost completely replaced the gaslights in cities, and they had begun to displace the age-old lamps and candles as well.

Progress in small towns and rural areas had to await improvements in the long-distance transmission of electrical power, but these too came rapidly. The electrification of America, indeed of most of the industrialized word, has to be counted as one of the greatest achievements of the first half of the twentieth century. It has probably altered our daily lives more profoundly than all the wars that were fought during the century.

Not only did electricity bring reliable and relatively cheap light into most homes, it also supplied the power to run everything from an electric hair dryer to a television set. The vacuum cleaner, the refrigerator, the air conditioner, and other devices that you use every day and without which life would be very much different and much harder than it is today, have all been made possible by electricity.

One hundred years ago, this source of power, which we now take for granted, was little more than a dream, a scientific curiosity shown only in a few laboratories.

6

Keeping It Clean and Neat

THE PATRONS OF a London restaurant on Victoria Street must have been shocked or at very least surprised when one of their fellow diners leaned over, put his lips to the plush seat on a chair, and began sucking at it. He then doubled over in a fit of choking and coughing as the dust filled his mouth and clogged his throat.

The man, whose named happened to be H. C. Booth, was not mad. He was an inventor, and he was testing the principle behind an invention he was working on. Booth's invention was to be called the vacuum cleaner.

This rather odd scene took place in the late nineteenth century. By 1901, Booth had patented his vacuum cleaner, but he wasn't the only one to hold a patent on this sort of device. As with most household inventions, the vacuum cleaner was being worked on by a number of different people over a fairly long period of time. So it is impossible to assign any one person complete credit for the invention.

A century ago most middle-class homes were heavily carpeted. Once a year, or perhaps more often, carpets were taken up, hung over a line in the backyard, and soundly beaten to get out the dust and accumulated grime. It was a reasonably effective though messy and time-consuming task. Carpets could also be sent to a commercial cleaner where the same sort of beating was done by machine.

By the 1860s, the carpet sweeper was in use. It had revolving brushes housed in a small chassis mounted on wheels or rollers. Carpet sweepers were still in wide use a century later and may still be used occasionally today. Despite its popularity and longevity, the carpet sweeper was not a particularly effective cleaner. Something more powerful was needed. And it was this need that prompted Mr. Booth to carry out his unusual experiment in the Victoria Street restaurant.

Booth's first practical vacuum cleaner was quite a bulky affair. It was pushed through the streets on a cart or truck and required a two-man crew to operate. People would bring rugs, chairs, and other household items out into the street to be cleaned when the vacuum cleaner truck came by. This vacuum cleaner was also extremely noisy and was not always appreciated, as Booth later recalled: "It was assumed by the police authorities that the machine [the vacuum cleaner] had no right to work on a public thoroughfare. . . . The Vacuum Cleaner Company was frequently sued for damages for alleged frightening of cab horses in the street."

In France large vacuum-cleaning machines were used in theaters to clean seats. Nevertheless, it was in America that the concept of cleaning by suction really took hold, though not at first as a portable vacuum cleaner.

In 1902, David T. Kenney installed a vacuum-cleaning system in the Frick Building in New York City. Within a very few years, the Kenney system was adapted for private homes as well. The motor for the system was quite large and was installed in the basement. Tubes ran from the motor to each room in the house. When cleaning was to be done, a flexible hose and nozzle were attached to the tube outlet in the room to be cleaned, and then the system was turned on. The dust was sucked down the tube into a receptacle in the basement. When another room was to be cleaned, the hose and nozzle were simply moved to that room. The system was efficient and very sturdy, but its cost was high. That is why it was only used in public buildings and the homes of the wealthy. It soon lost out completely to the portable vacuum cleaner. From time to time, one can still find the old stationary vacuum-cleaning system or its remains in homes built during the early 1900s.

Many different people were working on a portable vacuum cleaner, and they tried many different approaches. Who really "invented" the practical vacuum cleaner was a question fought out in the courts for years. Here too David T. Kenney came out on top and is generally given the bulk of the credit for the invention, particularly in America. Two basic types of vacuum cleaner emerged, and they are still with us today. The pure suction type is represented by the tank vacuum cleaners, and by the newly popular "electric broom." The handle type of vacuum cleaner combines the rotating brushes of the old carpet sweeper and suction. With attachments some early vacuum cleaners could also be used as blowers for drying hair.

Most American families acquired their first vacuum cleaner from an aggressive door-to-door salesman who generally sold the appliances on credit. Door-to-door selling was once much more common than it is today. The vacuum cleaner, because it was a fairly expensive, yet portable

Vacuum cleaner from the 1950s. The design of this appliance has changed very little over the years. (New York Public Library Picture Collection)

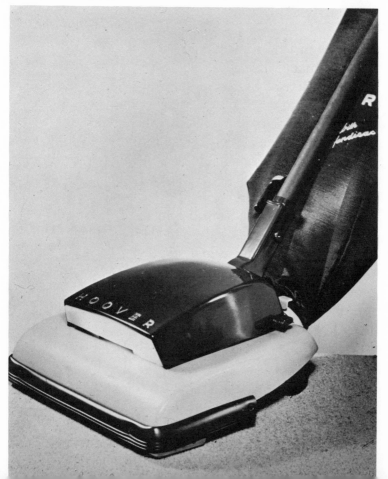

item, seemed to lend itself particularly well to this type of salesmanship. The new appliance was also taken up by the great mail-order houses such as Sears, Roebuck and Montgomery Ward, which were able to lower the prices, and make things tough for the door-to-door salesman.

While the vacuum cleaner still remained too expensive for poor families (many of whom didn't have electricity anyway), it became standard in most middle-class American homes by World War I, and it has changed very little since. The vacuum cleaner as pictured in the Sears catalog of 1917 is instantly recognizable. It would work pretty nearly as well as the vacuum cleaner you could buy out of this year's Sears catalog. The big difference is the price; in 1917 a vacuum cleaner cost $19.95.

Naturally there is a lot more to clean in the house than the carpets. Indeed, during the 1880s there was an incredible amount to clean. Many homes were under the influence of Victorian fashions, which called for heavily upholstered and intricately carved furniture, thick rugs and drapes, and rooms jammed to the bursting point with small ornamental objects. The Victorian room was a cleaning nightmare. To those who could afford to hire servants, that didn't make much difference. But most American households did not have servants, and the percentage that employed even part-time domestic help dropped steadily throughout the late nineteenth and early twentieth centuries. For the woman of the family even simple housework was an incredible chore leaving little time for anything else. If women were ever to be liberated from the endless task of washing and dusting, something had to be done about Victorian taste; by the end of the nineteenth century, the Victorian style was on its way out.

Health was another consideration in changing taste in the home. By the end of the nineteenth century, people had generally accepted the germ theory of disease. All those crevices and crannies, those plush fabrics and deep cushions so important to Victorian tastes were places where dust, dirt, and germs could hide. Ease of cleaning was not only liberating—it was sanitary.

In 1896, Mary Gay Humphreys wrote in the popular book *The House and Home*, "A busy woman is accustomed to say that her idea of the house of the future is one that can be cleaned with a hose." Though that never quite came about, there was a distinct movement on the part of those who designed homes and provided the interior decoration to make homes far simpler, and above all easier to clean.

Writes Gwendolyn Wright in *Building the Dream*,

> In the interest of eliminating unnecessary housework, an almost austere simplicity became the basis for domestic design. Uncluttered space and smooth surfaces were easier to clean. Instead of crevices or cornices, which had to be dusted, painted stencils began to adorn living rooms. New coverings in dyed cotton, jute, burlap, or recently improved rolls of wallpapers replaced carved or machine-made plaster ornament and walls often simply received a coat of smooth, white plaster. On the floor one found straw mats, small rag throw rugs, or the novel product called linoleum. Materials for walls and floors were supposed to be easy to wash and restful to gaze upon.

On the windows, newly popular and easier to clean venetian blinds replaced the heavy dust-catching draperies of earlier times. Where drapes and curtains remained, they were made of light and often nearly transparent materials.

Around the turn of the century, at a time when people were becoming interested in simpler and cleaner homes, people were also becoming interested in doing something about the deplorable conditions in which many of the poor, particularly the immigrant poor, of the cities lived. Very often the same people were interested in both causes. From the very best of motives, they tried to impose their standards of a clean uncluttered house upon people who didn't understand them and didn't want them.

There can be no question that the tenements in which the poor lived were more often than not hideous disease-producing horrors badly crowded and lacking adequate (or any) sanitation and washing facilities. It is also true that many of the poor were uneducated and simply did not comprehend the germ theory and the relationship between dirt and disease.

But for their part, the reformers often failed to appreciate and respect the tastes and desires of people who came from backgrounds very different from their own. The apartments of the immigrants were often cluttered, not only because they were overcrowded (which they certainly were) but also because the people who lived there liked heavy highly ornamented furniture, which was usually bought on the installment plan. Walls were covered with religious pictures or family photographs in fancy frames; if there was not enough money for frames, pictures were simply pasted to the wall. Bits and pieces of oddly matched wallpaper were stuck up, not just to cover the wall but to produce a highly colorful visual effect. In all of this the reformers saw only signs of ignorance and places where germs could hide and disease breed.

In 1904, a New York Tenement Investigation Committee suggested that all wallpaper should be removed from tenement apartments and its use prohibited in the future because germs and bugs lived in the layers of paper and paste. A commission appointed by President Theodore Roosevelt suggested that the poor should not be given ornamental furnishings because they harbored dust and germs.

But the furniture that the reformers saw only as cheap and gaudy dust catchers were objects of pride for their owners. These were things that they had worked for and wanted. The wallpaper and the pictures helped to relieve the visual dreariness of the tenement rooms. The reformers who thought only of keeping things clean were unable to see this or at least did not think it counted for much.

Much the same thoughtless passion for cleanliness and order carried over into the planning of housing for the poor in the twentieth century. The model company towns built for workers usually tried to impose an unnatural order and hygienic sameness on those who inhabited them. In public housing projects, residents couldn't hide a lot of junk behind closet doors. That's because doors were left off of closets so as to encourage neatness. There were regulations banning pets (dirty and noisy) and even regulations as to the color of paint on the walls (white or pale pastel shades preferred) and whether or not pictures could be hung. Such regulations showed little respect for the tastes and desires of the tenants. This patronizing attitude helped to contribute to the failure of so many public housing projects.

By the middle of the twentieth century, cleanliness and order had became an almost unassailable virtue for the American middle class, particularly for the middle-class housewife. Anything less than shining clean was supposed to be a sign of moral failure. Advertisers used this belief to work on the guilt feelings of the American housewife and sell her on an incredible (and highly profitable) collection of cleaning products and devices.

The appeal to guilt is exceptionally blatant in a 1928 advertisement in the *Ladies' Home Journal*, sponsored by an association of soap manufacturers.

The ad shows a concerned-looking wife and mother staring out of the window at a group of children playing in the yard. The headline reads, "What do the neighbors think of *her* children." The text continues:

> To every mother her own are the ideal children. But what do the neighbors think? Do *they* smile at happy, grimy faces acquired in wholesome play? For people have a way of associating unclean clothes and faces with other questionable characteristics.
>
> Fortunately, however, there's soap and water.
>
> "Bright shining faces" and freshly laundered clothes seem to make children welcome anywhere . . . and, in addition, speak volumes concerning their *parents'* personal habits as well.

The ad concludes "There's CHARACTER—in SOAP & WATER."

Though the technique is perhaps a bit crude and

unsophisticated for modern audiences, the basic appeal, that people will judge you on the cleanliness and order of your home and the personal appearance of your family, has changed hardly at all. Ads in which housewives are mortified by dusty furniture, dirty rugs, water-spotted glasses, floors that do not sparkle, clothes that are "dingy," and shirts with "ring around the collar" can be found on television every day.

As we can see, the cult of cleanliness extended to clothes. Getting clothes or other fabrics clean was an ancient problem. Washing was generally considered among the dirtiest and most disagreeable of all household tasks. A century ago, those who could afford to, sent their washing out to a laundress or washerwoman. In some cases, a hired washerwoman would come to a home weekly or twice a month to do the washing. The task was a backbreaking one using the technique that was first developed before the dawn of history. This consisted of taking the wet and soapy fabric and rubbing it vigorously against a rough object. By the nineteenth century, the washboard with its ribbed metal surface had become almost universal. The washing could be done in a washtub filled with water from a pump, in specially constructed washing sinks that were often found in the basements of homes and apartment buildings, or, if a home happened to have one, in the bathtub. The use of harsh soaps that could peel the skin off the user's hands added to the disagreeable nature of the task.

Attempts to mechanize this hard work go back at least to the beginning of the nineteenth century, but progress was extremely slow. Most of the early washing machines were large and cumbersome and apparently not

Glass Washboard. Will not rust or flatten; not affected by hot or cold water; is equally good for coarse or fine fabrics, 35c

Clothes Props, full size, 5c and 10c each; 50c and $1 a dozen

Curtain Stretcher, with hinge to prevent sagging; nickel pins; adjustable to curtains from two yards to four yards long, 75c; stretchers without pins, entirely new, $1.75 and $2; other stretchers up to $2.75

Washboards, zinc faced, full size, 15c to 65c

Clothes Pins in a box, 3 dozen, 5c

Clothes Hampers, $2.25 $2.75 $3.25 and $3.75; round hampers, special, $1

Washboards and other aids to home home laundering from John Wanamaker's 1901 catalog. (New York Public Library Picture Collection)

very effective. By about the 1850s, however, machines using a combination of steam and steam-powered rotating drums were developed. Such machines were far too large and too dangerous for household use, but they began to appear in commercial laundries. They remained the basic tool of commercial or "steam" laundries well into the twentieth century. Huge rollers or mangles powered first by steam and later by electricity were used to dry and take the wrinkles out of sheets, blankets, and other flat items.

Commercial laundries were used by hotels, hospitals, and other institutions, and some of them did business with the general public as well. These laundries got fabrics much cleaner than did the scrubbing on the old-fashioned washboard. But steam laundries were also notoriously hard on fabrics. Smaller "hand" laundries, which proliferated in cities during the early twentieth century, were somewhat better, but they too sometimes relied on the same sort of heavy-duty machinery. The results, all too often, were ripped and frayed sheets, missing buttons, and since all laundry tends to look pretty much alike, lost laundry. Then there was the expense. Though people who worked in laundries were among the lowest-paid workers, the cost of commercial laundering was still too steep for poorer families, particularly those with several children. Laundry to be "sent out" was limited to a few items such as a man's white dress shirts, which were difficult to clean and starch properly at home.

There was clearly a great need for a practical home washing machine, and inventors tried all sorts of approaches. Most early washing machines tried to imitate the rubbing and scrubbing motion of the washerwoman's knuckles against the washboard. One of the most successful applications of this technique was a curved tub in which fabrics were squeezed and pressed over a series of rollers. The machine was hand operated with a lever that was rocked back and forth. The basic prototype of this machine was patented before 1850, and as late as 1927, Montgomery Ward was still selling a hand-powered machine of that type, billed as "our famous 'Old Faithful.'" Faithful it may have been, but it represented only a slight improvement over the washboard, so most people didn't bother with it or any other washing machine. In 1912, a writer for *Ladies' Home Journal* could report that most washing in houses was still done without the aid of any sort of washing machine.

The basic mechanisms used in modern washing machines—the agitators, the revolving baskets, and the other

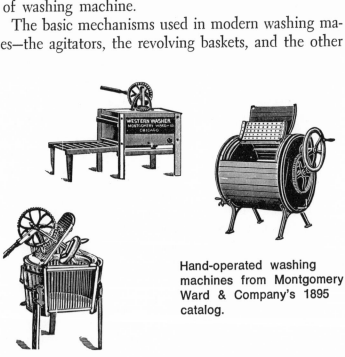

Hand-operated washing machines from Montgomery Ward & Company's 1895 catalog.

methods of forcing the soapy water through the fabric—were all well known a century and more ago. What was lacking was a reliable source of power to drive the machine. Electricity provided the source of power. Other prerequisites were reliable speed and time-changing mechanisms so that machines could be switched from the slow motion required by washing to the high speed needed in expelling water. By the 1920s, that problem too had been essentially solved, and the sales of electric washing machines rose dramatically. Over 1.4 million washing machines were sold in America in 1936. At the same time the average price of the machines dropped, from about $130 to $60, and in 1936, Ward's was able to offer an electric washing machine for a record low price of $29.95.

Still, even at that price there were many Americans who couldn't afford a washing machine. The Great Depression was in full swing. There were also a lot of families, particularly in rural areas, who didn't have electricity, so they couldn't use an electric washing machine anyway. Apartment dwellers had no place to put a washing machine, which required a hose to the sink for water and some sort of drain to carry away the waste water. Many apartment buildings had communal washing machines in the basement, and tenants did their washing according to an agreed-upon schedule. But even in 1936, the washboard was still a familiar item in most households, and people still sent shirts and other difficult items out to the "hand" laundry.

In the years following World War II, a new institution made its appearance on the American scene and spread rapidly, reaching practically every city and town in just a few years—it was the self-service laundry or launderette.

It consisted of rows of gleaming new washing machines where one could do a load of laundry for a quarter, or in some cases even a dime (in some places the price per load is now a dollar or more). Launderettes were more than just places to wash clothes. Because customers had to stand around for an hour or two while the machines washed and dried their clothes, the launderette took on the character of neighborhood social center as well. The launderette is still very much with us, though it is less common than it once was. The old "hand" laundry has almost entirely disappeared.

Many Americans first used new and more efficient types of washing machines in a launderette. As soon as they did, they wanted to have one of the machines in their own home where it could be used conveniently any hour of the day or night. Sales of washing machines soared in the postwar years. Soon, like the refrigerator and the stove, the washing machine became a standard house appliance. Even apartment dwellers tried to cram some sort of washing machine into their limited space. The day of the washboard was, at long last, over, or almost over.

Still, there were many fabrics, wool for example, that couldn't be thrown into the washing machine without courting disaster. Such fabrics required "dry" cleaning—that is, cleaning with something other than water, usually a fluid like naphtha, which not only gave off toxic fumes, but was highly flammable as well. The safest thing to do was to take such garments to a "dry" cleaner, a commercial establishment that specialized in cleaning woolens and other nonwashables. But dry cleaning was expensive, and in many families it was used only for special items—a man's business suit, for example, or a woman's best wool dress.

Everyday woolen items might be "dry-cleaned" at home with naphtha, a dangerously explosive fluid.

Dry cleaners have not disappeared, as have most "hand" laundries, but they are not as numerous as they once were. The main reason for their decline is that more and more fabrics today are machine-washable. Self-service dry cleaning, where the customer is charged by the pound rather than by the garment, has never really caught on. The price of that kind of cleaning is lower, but most people seem to prefer clothes that are machine-washable.

After an item is washed, it has to be dried, and the time-honored way of doing that is hanging it out in the sun. But even before it can be hung out to dry, the excess water has to be squeezed out of it. The washerwoman did this by twisting—literally wringing the water out. Early washing machines both hand operated and electric had attached wringers, a pair of hard rubber rollers that pressed the excess water out of the fabric. Hand-cranked wringers were sometimes sold separately to be used in conjunction with the washboard. Modern washing machines spin the clothes partially dry, thus entirely eliminating the need for the wringer.

And then the clothes were hung out to dry on a line in the backyard if one happened to have a backyard or simply out the window if there were no backyards. On sunny days, many poorer apartment buildings could be nearly obscured by laundry drying on lines attached to fire escapes, trees, telephone poles, or just about anything. Sheets and overalls flapping in the breeze were among the most familiar urban sights for much of the twentieth century.

But what was one to do on days that weren't sunny,

or during the winter months when clothes would freeze on the line? First, you didn't wash clothes as often. Second, you tried to dry them somewhere inside. Many private homes had a room set aside for drying, usually a room near the furnace where clothes could dry more quickly in the heat. Small apartment buildings had indoor lines in the basement for drying, though it sometimes took days to dry an item that would have dried outside in a few hours. Even then clothes seemed damp and had to be dried again on the radiator. There were a variety of clothes bars and curtain stretchers for indoor drying. And in a pinch one of the contraptions could be set up in the bathroom, kitchen, living room, or anywhere else where there was a bit of space. A prolonged rainy spell often meant that a house or apartment would be filled with damp clothes hung out to dry.

The solution to this problem was a machine to dry clothes as well as wash them. But the dryer is a relatively late entry into the average home. The principle is quite simple: the clothes are rotated inside a heated drum. Gas-fired dryers were sometimes used in commercial laundries, although the heat was high and they tended to be pretty hard on clothes. When launderettes sprang up, they generally had dryers as well as washing machines. This created a demand for home dryers as well as washers. Soon a washer-dryer combination became a standard feature for new homes. The tremendous increase in energy costs during the 1970s has given line drying a renewed popularity, but it has not ushered in a renaissance for the washboard.

After clothes were washed and dried, they had to be ironed, a task considered, next to washing itself, the most horrible of household duties. The flatiron is basically a

A compact version of the modern washer-dryer combination.
(General Electric)

thick piece of metal that is heated and then pressed over a fabric, usually a damp fabric, to keep it from scorching. The trouble was that there was no way of really controlling the heat. The iron had to be reheated every ten minutes or so. In the warmer months, the stove or other heat source that had to keep the flatiron warm would also turn any room into a furnace. What was needed was an iron with its own internal and consistent heat source.

In the 1850s, a gas-heated iron was introduced. It consisted of a flexible tube attached to a gas jet on one end and a hollow iron on the other. The iron was heated by a gas-fed flame. This sort of ironing was probably a fairly dangerous process because of the risk of gas fire and explosion. The gas iron never really caught on.

The large twin rollers or mangles used by commercial laundries were adapted for home use, and the Ward's catalog of 1905 offered the "Household Favorite Ironer," which was turned by hand and had a heated metal roller.

But the stove-heated flatiron remained the basic household ironing tool until the introduction of the electric iron during the early years of the twentieth century. Electric flatirons first came on the market around 1909. In the 1920s, the rotary type of ironer was also electrified and hailed as a great advance in freedom for women. In 1922, a writer for *Good Housekeeping* upbraided the American housewife, "You may say you do not use the old type of flat iron, that you use an electric iron; that indeed is one step in advance. Even that is inefficient. Now isn't it foolish to iron a tablecloth, an area of about 18,000 square inches, with a heated tool measuring only 24 inches." The electric ironer was designed to change all of that. A sheet of tablecloth could be passed through the rollers and ironed in

Housekeeping Helps that you should have

For quicker, easier ironing — the "American Beauty" Electric Iron. Making its own heat, inside, one iron does all the work — saves time and steps; stays clean; heating-element guaranteed for all time.

Price $5—anywhere in the United States.

Toast to your taste, at table, with the "American" Electric Toaster. It makes delicious, crisp, tender, evenly browned toast — is light, unbreakable, economical.

Price $4—anywhere in the United States.

Get them at your electric supply, hardware or department store, or order from us direct—carriage prepaid upon receipt of price. Canadian prices add duty.

Full descriptions of the above and many other "American" electric heating-devices in free booklet: "Heat without Fire." Write for it today.

American Electrical Heater Company

Oldest and Largest Exclusive Makers
1345 Woodward Avenue
Detroit, U. S. A.

Advertisement for an electric iron in 1912. Note the electric toaster also. (New York Public Library Picture Collection) seconds, and the housewife could sit down while doing the job.

The first household electric ironers were cumbersome, expensive, and sometimes dangerous devices, but they improved rapidly. Cheaper portable models were developed. In the years that followed World War II, the electric ironer was one of those new household appliances that one *had* to have. During the 1950s, the electric ironer with its rollers abruptly disappeared. A person growing up in America during the last twenty or so years has probably never seen one of these appliances except perhaps stuck away and gathering dust in an attic or basement. What killed them off was a change of habits. They had been designed to iron sheets, tablecloths, curtains, all large flat items, although they could also be used for men's underwear and pajamas. To many housewives of the pre–World War II generation, unironed sheets or pajamas seemed almost sinful. But their daughters found that sheets that had been properly dried on the line or in the machine were relatively wrinkle free, and ironing underwear was superfluous. Besides, new fabrics made ironing far less necessary. So the electric ironer, once hailed as a great liberator of the housewife, was made obsolete by the housewife's liberation from ironing entirely. Well, not completely. For a while there seemed to be the promise that synthetic fabrics would completely eliminate the need for ironing, but that has never quite worked out. The electric flatiron, now modified with a variety of temperature settings and sprays, is still found in every home. But what was once one of the worst household tasks has now been reduced to a relatively minor annoyance.

7

Home Entertainment

THERE WAS NO instrument more particular to home entertainment a century ago than the stereoscope. This curious-looking device came in a variety of shapes and sizes. Basically it consisted of a couple of eyepieces. Sticking out in front of the eyepieces was a rod, and at the end of the rod was a small rack. Into the rack was placed a piece of thick cardboard with two nearly identical pictures on it. When one looked through the eyepieces, the picture appeared as a single three-dimensional image.

Staring at three-dimensional still pictures will not strike a person living in the late twentieth century as a particularly exciting form of entertainment. But what a marvel it seemed a hundred years ago. Photography had already been around for nearly half a century, but photographs could not yet be reproduced in newspapers or magazines. There were, of course, no motion pictures or television yet. The only photographs a person was likely to see were prints—usually family pictures. To see pictures in three dimensions seemed wonderful indeed.

What scenes did people want to look at? The Ward's 1895 catalog offers quite an assortment. Being a Chicago-based company, many of the stereoscopic views listed by Ward's had a Chicago connection. The catalog also offered prospective buyers views of Yellowstone National Park and other Western scenes, Scandinavian scenery, Alaskan landscapes, and views "of the ruins of Johnstown Pa. and Conemaugh valley. The greatest casualty in American history." These last were disaster pictures from the Johnstown flood of 1889.

With the stereoscope, people were able to see scenes and places that they would never have been able to see

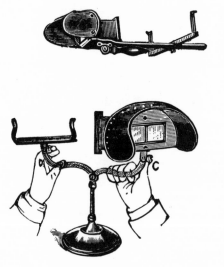

Stereoscopes offered in Montgomery Ward & Company's 1895 catalog.

in the normal course of their lifetime. Thus this rather absurd, Victorian-looking instrument was an important source of information as well as of entertainment.

One hundred years ago if you wanted to hear music in your home, you pretty well had to make it yourself. A piano or organ was a standard feature of the middle-class home. Also standard was one or more family members who knew how to play the instrument. Gathering around the piano to sing the latest popular songs like "Daisy Bell" or "On the Banks of the Wabash" from sheet music was a common evening pastime. Accordions, banjos, harmonicas, and even the humble ocarina or "musical sweet potato" were to be found in many homes. Children learned how to play these instruments for themselves, and if they showed any talent, they played for others.

The automatic player piano, or pianola, first appeared on the scene around 1900. It employed a roll of perforated paper that moved the hammers of the piano, which in turn struck the notes on the keyboard. In principle, it was a gigantic music box. The pianola was large, expensive, and limited in the range of music it could play, but it enjoyed a considerable popularity during the early decades of the twentieth century. As with an ordinary piano, family and friends could gather around to sing along with the music, but it was no longer necessary to find someone who knew how to play the piano. All one had to do was sit on the stool and push the pedals to operate the device. And unlike Aunt Tillie, the player piano struck all the right notes.

By the 1920s, the popularity of the player piano was already in decline. Although in the 1960s the player piano did enjoy a revival in popularity, it was more as a historical oddity than as a serious home entertainment medium. Besides, the late twentieth century models were electrified. What caused the decline in the use of the player piano was the improvement and diffusion of an invention that had already been around for a long time—the phonograph.

The invention of the phonograph is generally credited to Thomas A. Edison. Around the turn of the century Edison was, in many respects, the quintessential American hero. He was an inventive genius, yet a practical man as well. There was nothing theoretical or abstract about Edison's genius. He unashamedly invented for the marketplace. Along with his undoubted inventive genius, Edison also possessed a genius for self-promotion. Thus the legend has come down to us that Thomas A. Edison was the sole inventor of the phonograph. That is not quite accurate, although Edison certainly made an extremely important contribution to the development of the phonograph. He also coined the name.

The theory behind the phonograph—that a permanent record could be made of sound waves—had been practically demonstrated as early as 1857. What Edison did was develop an instrument that not only recorded the sound waves, but was able to play them back. Edison and his associates had experimented with the idea of the phonograph throughout much of 1877, and by early 1878 Edison was able to secure a patent on the device and to give public demonstrations. These turned out to be absolute sensations.

Edison biographer Robert Conot writes of an early demonstration:

> An awful hush preceded the demonstration. "The Speaking Phonograph has the honor of presenting it-

self to the Academy of Sciences," a metallic voice uttered from the instrument. Following that introduction, Batchelor [an Edison associate] shouted, sang, whistled and crowed like a rooster into the diaphragm. When the machine repeated the sounds, two or three girls in the audience fainted.

The whole thing seemed so astonishing that a couple of scientists publicly declared that Edison's talking phonograph was nothing but a fraud and a trick and that the inventor was an exceptionally gifted ventriloquist! It wasn't a trick, but it wasn't practical for home use either. Edison's first phonograph employed a tinfoil-covered cylinder. The grooves that stored and reproduced the sound were etched into the tinfoil. Once the initial astonishment wore off, what became obvious was that the quality of sound reproduction was pretty poor. So Edison and his team went to work trying to improve the sound quality.

Legend has it that the first recorded words were the nursery rhyme "Mary had a little lamb." According to Conot, this nursery rhyme was used but often with variations considered shocking at the time. An early recording contains this one:

"Mary has a new sheath gown, It is too tight by half. Who cares a damn for Mary's lamb, When they can see her calf!"

Edison did not at first see the phonograph as an entertainment device. He suggested it be used in clocks and watches for calling out the time and for delivering recorded advertisements. When Edison was working on the phonograph, the Statue of Liberty was going up in New York Harbor and the inventor suggested that a phonograph be put inside so that the "Goddess of Liberty" could be heard talking and whistling all over New York Harbor. Fortunately this Edison dream was never fulfilled.

Problems continued to plague Edison's phonograph after its startlingly sensational introduction. The biggest problem was the medium on which the sound was recorded. Tinfoil simply did not produce very good quality recordings, and it was delicate. After a few replays the tinfoil was useless. Edison tried a frustratingly large number of other recording mediums without much success before he turned his restless energies to other projects including what was to be his most successful invention, the electric light bulb. For years Edison's phonograph languished.

Others, notably telephone inventor Alexander Graham Bell, took up the sound reproduction project, and by the late 1880s, a wax cylinder was being used to record voices and music with far greater fidelity than anything Edison had been able to come up with. But still the machine was not practical for home use.

In the late 1880s, Edison finally turned his attention back to the phonograph. In 1889, after a series of difficult experiments and even more difficult financial and business arrangements, Edison announced that he had developed the "perfect phonograph." Well, it wasn't quite perfect, though it was a good deal better than what had gone before. It was also a good deal more expensive than competing types of "talking machines." Edison's problem here sprang in large part from his growing commitment to electricity. While other inventors were working on machines that were spring powered and that the user would simply wind up, Edison insisted on an electrically driven machine. In 1889, that meant a battery-powered phonograph. The whole complex and expensive contraption, battery included, weighed about one hundred pounds, and the battery only lasted about ten hours. Outraged buyers complained that the battery always seemed to give out right in the middle of a performance for friends. Edison was deluged with angry letters.

Edison's machine was no match for devices like the windup "Graphophone," which Sears was selling for a modest $18.75. Sears also offered a dozen of their "best and loudest records" for $5.00. The mail-order house advertised its machines both for home use and for giving public demonstrations. The 1900 catalog assured customers that they could make from $5.00 to $25.00 a night giving exhibitions of the marvelous talking machine in halls, churches, schoolhouses, and the like.

During the early decades of the twentieth century, the windup phonograph in one form or another was the one to be found in most homes. But ultimately Edison's faith in the future of electricity proved to be justified. As electrification of homes spread so did the electric phonograph, finally displacing the windup variety.

Another innovation, not Edison's this time, was the use of the flat disc for recording. Edison had used a cylinder, but the disc developed by the German-born inventor Emile Berliner was far superior in a variety of ways. Sound reproduction quality was better, it was easier to handle and manufacture, and recordings could be made on both sides. Berliner called his machine the Gramophone, and he actually began small-scale manufacture in 1894. Berliner and his associates improved not only the record, but the machine itself. They concentrated on the clockwork-driven windup machine. In 1901, they formed what was called the Victor Talking Machine Company. Their windup device, now popularly known as the Victrola, became the most popular of all phonographs in the early twentieth century.

A highly successful advertising campaign of the 1920s asked the question, "What Will You Do on Those Long Shivery Evenings"—the answer was stay home and listen to your Victrola.

The sound quality of a 1920s record might make a present-day audiophile cover his or her ears in shock and horror. But a record of that era, played on a good Victrola, produced a reasonably faithful approximation of both instrumental music and the human voice. The great success of the phonograph brought about a major change in the way people entertained themselves. They could now hear singers and instrumentalists they could never have hoped to hear live. The phonograph also released people from the need and the pleasure of making their own music. At one time it was thought necessary for someone in the family to be able to play the piano or some other instrument with reasonable skill. With the rise of the phonograph, all the skill anyone needed to make music was to be able to put a needle on a record.

The early Edison machine was used equally for playing and recording. And the "talking machine" advertised in the 1900 Sears catalog was touted as "A Machine Which Will Record or Make Records As Well As Reproduce Them." As the technology of recording advanced, these two functions were separated, and only records that were prerecorded were available for home use. The technology of making recordings had become too complex for the home.

During World War II, little recording studios for the general public sprang up. It was possible for a serviceman to make a brief recording of his voice. The recording was then mailed back to the folks at home. After the war, simple voice recordings could be made in coin-operated booths. But this was inconvenient, the quality was poor, and the price comparatively high, so making your own "records" was never much more than a gimmick.

Home recording was introduced, or rather reintroduced, first with the wire recorder, which as the name implies, made its recordings on wire, and then with the tape recorder. For a while it appeared as if tape might actually replace records as the primary recording medium. But that has never quite happened, or it hasn't happened yet, for most people still find records more convenient to use and feel that they produce a better quality of sound. However, the quality of tape is improving all the time, and the balance may shift.

The phonograph has always been primarily a means of home entertainment. The radio was that and more—a good deal more. It became a channel for mass education, information, and persuasion.

Early radio is identified with the name of the Italian inventor Guglielmo Marconi, but Marconi isn't really the "inventor" of radio. The scientific principles behind it had been known for a long time. Like Edison, Marconi was as much of an entrepreneur and a promoter as he was an inventor. It was Marconi who first convinced a generally skeptical world of the practicality of the "wireless." This he did in 1899 by broadcasting "wireless" telegraph messages across the English Channel.

The wireless was first used for communicating with

ships at sea and for long-distance communication of private messages like the telegraph system of a generation earlier. The "wireless" first entered the home in the hands of amateurs who were enthralled by the new technology and enjoyed sending messages to one another. It wasn't until the 1920s that broadcasting to a mass audience really began to have an impact. By 1929, there were some nine to ten million radio sets in the United States. A witness before the House Merchant Marine Committee in 1929 called radio, "God's greatest gift to the twentieth century."

March 1929 saw a milestone for radio, a broadcast of the inauguration of President Herbert Hoover. It wasn't the first broadcast of an inauguration; four years earlier there had been a radio description of the Coolidge inauguration. But in 1925, radio was still a novelty, and the sets were much too expensive for the average family. By 1929, the infant industry had grown enormously. So had the sophistication of broadcasting. Whereas the 1925 inauguration had been broadcast from a single location, the 1929 inauguration coverage was switched from one spot to another.

In *1929: America Before the Crash*, author Warren Sloat explains how this broadcast sounded to listeners throughout the world.

> Graham McNamee of NBC took his microphone with him into the sentry box at the north portico of the White House, describing the callers as they arrived to bid good-bye to the departing President. Then NBC switched to an announcer flying over the Washington Monument. They heard a description of President and Mrs. Coolidge leaving the White House, then heard

crowds cheering Hoover as he appeared in the street. They heard a corps of announcers describe the parade's formation and procession—some at vantage points along Pennsylvania Avenue, some at the Peace Monument, some from a booth on the Treasury steps. A microphone was poised near Hoover as Chief Justice William Howard Taft administered the affirmation of office. . . . They heard the first broadcast ever of a vice-president being sworn to office in the Senate Chamber. They even heard a transcontinental transmission; The program was switched to Palo Alto, California, where the Stanford University orchestra and chorus serenaded two of its graduates, the President and the First Lady, at lunch a continent away.

It was estimated that some 63 million people around the world heard parts of the daylong broadcast. The voice of radio reached as far as the frozen continent of Antarctica where an American expedition under Admiral Richard E. Byrd was encamped.

Radio receivers were set up in public auditoriums. People went to restaurants and bars that had radios. Radios in schools were turned to the inauguration. But most people listened in their homes, and they invited in neighbors who didn't have radios of their own.

Radio began to play an increasingly large part in the lives of most Americans, indeed in the lives of most people in the industrialized world. While Herbert Hoover merely had his inauguration broadcast, his successor, Franklin D. Roosevelt, made use of the radio as a powerful political tool. He communicated directly with the American people through his enormously effective "fireside chats." In truth,

A radio broadcast in 1931. (Columbia Broadcasting Company)

there was no fireplace, only a microphone, but the fireplace has always been a powerful symbol of domesticity in America. The American public came to be familiar not only with FDR's face, from photographs and newsreels, but with his voice as well.

As World War II began in Europe, the drama of the conflict was brought right into American living rooms by newsman Edward R. Murrow's broadcasts from London. When America entered the war after the attack on Pearl Harbor in 1941, Americans first turned to their radios not their newspapers for information about the conflict. Families gathered around the radio each evening to get the war news from Europe and the Pacific.

But it wasn't just news that people wanted to hear on the radio. Except during the war years, radio was primarily an entertainment medium. In the afternoons housewives tuned into such soap operas as "Stella Dallas," "Our Gal Sunday," and "The Romance of Helen Trent." Although most radio soaps were broadcast out of New York City, they were generally given a small-town background. Radio soaps never dealt frankly with subjects like sex, but still the plots and general feel of the radio soaps would be quite familiar to the watcher of today's popular televised soap operas. The name *soap opera*, by the way, comes from the fact that many of these daytime radio melodramas were originally sponsored by soap companies.

Late afternoon and early evening on the radio was dominated by kids shows, usually adventure serials like "The Lone Ranger" and "Jack Armstrong, All American Boy." Evenings were given over to family entertainment, dramas like "The Philip Morris Playhouse," which often featured name actors from the movies, comedy-variety shows hosted by the likes of Jack Benny, Bob Hope, and Eddie Cantor, and musical shows with orchestras like those of Guy Lombardo, Wayne King, and Kay Kyser.

Most early radio shows were broadcast live. But the big nationwide network shows were increasingly prerecorded.

Radio entertainment reached the height of its popularity in the years immediately following World War II.

However, the technology for radio's displacement as the leading medium for entertainment and information was already well advanced. The new development was, of course, television.

Workable television systems were already being demonstrated in the 1930s. As with other technology, there was a time lag between development and practical application. The advance in television was stopped dead by World War II. After the war, television advanced rapidly. There were a million TV receivers in use in 1949. Two years later that number had doubled, and by the end of the decade of the 1950s over 50 million television sets were in operation in the United States.

Forests of unsightly TV antennas sprouted atop private homes and apartment buildings. Early television sets showed fuzzy black and white pictures on small screens. The first commercial sets had screens only about seven inches across.

Not only were the screens small, during the late 1940s, there wasn't much to see anyway. Here is the lineup for a typical TV day in April 1948 on New York's WABD, Channel 5. Programming didn't even begin until six in the evening, and after the playing of "The Star-Spangled Banner," people would see the weather report. This was followed at 6:15 P.M. by "The Small Fry Club," then came half an hour of news from Washington, D.C. The remainder of the evening's programming was made up primarily of film shorts, the kind of material that otherwise was used to fill in time at movie theaters. The final program, boxing from Jamaica Arena, began at 9 P.M. When the match was over, so was broadcasting for the day.

Since the price of a television set was extremely high,

well beyond the budget of an average family, most people first watched television in an appliance shop window or in a bar. Television became a major attraction for bars, and television programmers responded by scheduling a high percentage of sports during their limited hours of broadcasting.

Early television created popularity for a couple of otherwise obscure sports. One was professional wrestling, not really a sport at all, but a sort of bizarre show where huge and strangely dressed men pretended to beat one another to a pulp while spectators screamed and threw things into the ring. One of the earliest TV stars was a wrestler called Gorgeous George, who had garishly bleached and curled hair and entered the ring preceded by a valet spraying the place with perfume. Another popular early TV sport was the roller derby. Teams of men and women on skates raced madly around a rink, regularly elbowing, kicking, shoving, and biting one another in order to get ahead. Good taste was not a prominent feature of early TV.

For those who didn't like wrestling or roller derby, and even for many who did, there was the "Texaco Star Theater" with comedian Milton Berle. Berle's show began in the 1948–49 season and rapidly became something of a national obsession. Every Tuesday night at 8 P.M. people all over America would try to find a television set in order to watch "Uncle Miltie," a onetime burlesque comedian, get hit with pies or romp around dressed as a chicken. Berle quickly became the "King of Television." His success persuaded advertisers to buy time on the new medium, induced stars from the stage and screen to give TV a try, and most of all, convinced ordinary people that no matter what the price and no matter how poor the quality of the picture a TV set was something well worth having in the living room.

The 1950s ushered in what has been called the Golden Age of Television. Comedians who had become famous on the radio or screen like Jack Benny, Fred Allen, and Abbott and Costello began appearing regularly on television. Television also began to create its own stars. Two unknown comedians, Sid Caesar and Imogene Coca, did a weekly 90-minute comedy-variety show called "Your Show of Shows." The show is still remembered fondly today by those who grew up with it. There was drama too —live television drama such as "Studio One," "The Kraft Theatre," and "The Philco Television Playhouse." These shows attracted well-known actors. Humphrey Bogart, Lauren Bacall, and Henry Fonda appeared in a televised version of the play *The Petrified Forest* in 1955. It was Bogie's only live TV appearance. Sir Laurence Olivier starred in *The Moon and Sixpence* and Mary Martin did *Peter Pan*. Television also began to create some of its own dramatic stars. Paul Newman got his acting or rather his singing start in a televised musical version of *Our Town*. The established star of that particular production was Frank Sinatra.

Today this era is looked back upon nostalgically, as a great and creative time in television history. Were the shows really as good as some remember them to be? In many cases, we will never know, for most were not recorded. But some bits from this era have been preserved, if only on scratchy kinescope recordings. Not long ago, some sketches from Sid Caesar and Imogene Coca's show "Your Show of Shows" were put together and shown in movie theaters and later on television. Public broadcasting also dug up old kinescopes of some of the famous original TV dramas like Paddy Chayevsky's *Marty*. A quarter century later these shows did not seem quite as good as some remembered them, but they were still good.

With all of that good entertainment coming into the living room—for free—people wondered why they should bother to leave home in order to pay to sit in an uncomfortable movie theater. And in large numbers they rapidly decided that there was no reason at all (except during the summer, for theaters had air conditioning). People stayed home, and with the money they saved by not going to the movies, they bought television sets.

The sets themselves improved. Screens went from seven to ten to twelve to nineteen inches across. In many areas, the expensive and unsightly outdoor antennas were no longer needed. Viewers were able to get along with indoor TV antennas—rabbit ears as they were often called —a semicircular base with two telescopic extensions. A great deal of viewing time was spent fiddling with the antenna, turning it this way and that in order to reduce the "snow" or get rid of the "ghost" in the picture. With all its inconvenience, the influence of television was growing.

Television was having its impact in other ways. In 1954, a senator from Wisconsin named Joseph McCarthy said that the United States Army was riddled with Communist infiltrators. A series of congressional hearings was scheduled to air this charge. ABC television, which had no important daytime programming in 1954, asked McCarthy if they could bring cameras into the hearing room and televise the hearings live.

In Max Wilk's *The Golden Age of Television*, Robert Kintner, who was at the time head of ABC-TV programming, recalled:

> McCarthy was all for it. I don't think he had the vaguest idea what was going to happen to him. From then on, we televised every day, and as McCarthy and Joseph Welch, the Boston lawyer, began to grapple with each other in the hearing room, it drew enormous attention. . . . The end result of those hearings on television is now history. The huge power of television coverage of live news events was demonstrated beyond any doubt—much, much stronger than any sort of live entertainment programming that could be done from a network studio. The mass impact of those hearings really did destroy McCarthy's career; after his confrontation with Welch, he began to go downhill very rapidly.

President Dwight Eisenhower hired actor Robert Montgomery to act as his TV consultant. There were a lot of jokes at the time about hiring an actor to help a president.

Still, as late as 1960, the tremendous impact of television in the home was not fully realized by most politicians. During that year's presidential campaign, a televised debate between the two candidates, Democrat John F. Kennedy and Republican Richard M. Nixon, was proposed. Both accepted, but Kennedy apparently did not take the debate very seriously. He thought the election would be decided in the newspapers and weekly news magazines. Serious or not, Kennedy was a clear winner in the debates, not so much because of his debating skill (which was considerable) but because of his appearance and air of confidence. Under the harsh television lights Nixon looked bad —shifty eyed and unshaven. Most political commentators called the Kennedy-Nixon debates the turning point in the election, which resulted in a narrow Kennedy victory. Once in office, Kennedy quickly appreciated the power of television and with his televised news conferences became the first real television-age president. Three years after the election of John F. Kennedy, the people of America sat glued to their television sets for up-to-the-minute news of the assassination of that president. And a few days later, millions watched in horror as the president's presumed assassin, Lee Harvey Oswald, was himself assassinated before live television cameras.

Live and taped TV coverage of the war in Vietnam profoundly altered the way most people thought about that war. Terrorists have at times actually staged events for television—the massacre of the Israeli athletes at the Munich Olympics in 1972, for example. Television brought the world into people's homes, even if they didn't want it.

All that time, television itself was changing. By the 1970s, the prices of TV sets had dropped to the point where practically everyone could afford one. The person who resisted TV was considered something of an eccentric. Color TV had been introduced, first in expensive, difficult-to-operate sets, but gradually both the price and quality improved, and color TV is now the standard.

TV progressed from the early era of forests of outside antennas, then to the inside "rabbit ears." In the 1980s, television entered the age of the cable. The cable not only produces clearer pictures but also gives the viewer access to an enormous number of TV channels. There are now special channels devoted to movies, to news, to sports,

Today's video projection systems can produce wall-sized TV pictures. (Sony Corporation of America)

to business, to the arts. There are channels for "adult entertainment" and for religious programming. Microwave and satellite transmission of TV programs will further expand the number of channels available in the future.

And there is more. With the addition of a video recorder, viewers can now record TV programs, even TV programs that they didn't watch. Prerecorded movies that can be shown on the home television set are available both on tapes and discs.

And there is still more—the hottest "toy" during the early 1980s was the video game. A small computer is hooked up to the TV set. A cartridge program is inserted, and a game appears on the home TV screen. This burgeon-

Atari's popular video computer system for playing video games and some of the game cartridges that it uses. (Atari)

ing business began in 1975 with Pong, a game in which an electric "ball" was batted back and forth across the TV screen by electronic "paddles," which could be controlled by the players. Year by year the games have increased in number, sophistication, and popularity.

With video recorders and game attachments, the television set is now often called a "home entertainment center."

No area of home life has changed more dramatically or completely over the last one hundred years. Remember a century ago home entertainment meant stereoscope slides and singing "Daisy Bell" around the piano.

8

The Great Mail-Order Merchants

WHERE DID IT all come from, the flood of new items that have poured into the home year after year over the past one hundred years? Perhaps no century in human history has presented the average person with more different kinds of items that could be purchased. Where did people buy them? How did they know what to buy?

One hundred years ago many people who lived in cities bought their household goods in department stores, just as most of us do today. But remember, a century ago the majority of people in America didn't live in cities. America was a predominantly rural country. Many farm families didn't even live near a small town. They had limited access to large stores, and many had never visited a department store in their lives. There were trains, but in the country the main method of transportation was still the horse and wagon.

Small towns had their stores—dry goods stores, hardware stores. Larger towns also had specialty stores such as those that sold furniture. But the stock of these merchants was, of necessity, limited. They didn't have the space to keep a large number of different items on hand. And what if a product didn't sell? The merchant was stuck with it, and a merchant couldn't afford that to happen too often and expect to stay in business. Stock was all too often slow in arriving at the store. For farmers, who often lived miles from the nearest store, which had to be reached on horseback, shopping was far from convenient.

The farmers' life was from time to time enlivened by a visit from a traveling salesman, who carried a line of wares in his wagon or, where trains were accessible, in his large suitcase. But a wagon could hold only so much, and a suitcase held even less. Traveling salesmen often carried only samples, the products themselves were ordered and shipped at a later date. Besides, the traveling salesman did not have the best of reputations in America. A traveling salesman sold his items, and the next day he was gone. If the product was no good, the purchaser often had no recourse. Salesmen were also relatively sophisticated when compared to the farmer. All those old jokes about the traveling salesman and the farmer's daughter may not have been justified, but they did express a general national attitude toward the traveling salesman as a slick-talking and immoral con man. In cities, door-to-door salesmen sold a particular item or line of goods, brushes and later vacuum cleaners, for example.

About one hundred years ago, a new method of shopping began to take hold in America. It was called mail-order shopping. The customer would send in an order by mail to a central location. The order would be filled and shipped directly to the customer. Actually mail-order shopping had begun in New England on a very small scale as early as 1830. By the 1880s, there were hundreds of small mail-order houses throughout the country. The products were not delivered to the door by the mailman. For farmers, there was no door-to-door mail service until 1896, and there was no parcel post for anyone until 1913. Only the orders were sent by mail. The products were generally shipped by rail express and customers picked them up at the freight office. The post office and the freight office may have been a lot closer and more convenient for the farmer than the nearest dry goods store. Customers were able to order items by mail that the local merchant did not stock.

Aaron Montgomery Ward, a former dry goods store manager and traveling salesman, was the first to try and expand the potential of mail-order selling to provide products that "could fill the needs of all members of the rural family from grandma to the family dog." Ward opened the first large mail-order house in America in 1872.

Ward saw a number of advantages in mail-order selling. Primarily he could sell goods more cheaply through the mail because he eliminated the middleman—the jobber who bought goods from the manufacturer and sold them to the store, which in turn sold them to the customer. The middleman had to make his own profit, and that upped the ultimate cost of the goods. Ward bought directly from the manufacturer, and he bought and sold in quantity, which also lowered the price.

Another money-saving practice was that Ward's sold only for cash. The customer sent in the money or paid for the order at the freight office when he or she picked it up.

There were no interest charges, no bad credit risks. This too tended to lower the cost of the goods.

But the most significant thing about Montgomery Ward's mail-order house was that he could offer his customers a huge assortment of goods. The local dry goods store could not possibly stock a large selection of silks, saddles, and stoves under a single roof—but Ward's could. And all of these were offered at better prices than the local merchant could give. No wonder small merchants hated the giant mail-order houses. They coined terms like "Monkey" Ward for Montgomery Ward, and "Rears and Soreback" for the biggest mail-order house of all, Sears, Roebuck. The insults didn't trouble the mail-order giants, who continued to prosper.

The main tool of Montgomery Ward's salesmanship was the catalog. When Ward started in 1872, his "catalog" was a single sheet listing the items for sale and information on how to order them. Two years later, the single sheet had grown into an eight-page booklet. In 1884, the Ward's catalog contained 240 pages listing nearly 10,000 items, each item or class of items illustrated by a woodcut. Wards proclaimed itself to be "the cheapest cash house in the country."

The mail-order catalog, which had been developed as a selling tool, became an instrument for social change as well. In most societies change comes very slowly. People, particularly those who live in rural areas, tend to resist change and innovation. In the days before radio and television, when most travel was by wagon or horseback and a long-distance train ride a rarity, people were often unaware of changes that were taking place elsewhere.

The mail-order catalog reached the home of the most

WHAT ONE GETS

Is measured to a great extent by what one goes after. Go after the right thing in the right way and you are fairly sure of right results.

There is such a thing as going after the right thing the wrong way, or the wrong thing the right way. Be careful not to fall into these too common errors.

The way to make a saving in purchasing your necessities of life is to write us for freight rates from Chicago to your town, figure up our prices as per quotations in our various catalogues, compare the *total* with the *total* cost of the same goods if purchased from your local dealers. This is the right way, and we feel sure of getting our share of your trade if you will do as we suggest.

Judicious buying means money in the savings bank.

CHICAGO.

This statement from a Montgomery Ward catalog explains how to save money by ordering by mail.

isolated farmer. It put into the hands of the farm family an enormous list of available products, things they could actually buy, if they had the money. As the farm family pored over the twice-yearly Ward's catalog, they could see what new items were being offered, what other people were buying. There were the obvious changes in fashions in clothes, but there were also changes in stoves, bathtubs, and washing machines. Many American families purchased their first phonograph or refrigerator through a mail-order catalog.

As they turned the pages of the increasingly bulky catalogs, families saw not only what they were going to buy right away, but also what items they would want and plan to buy in the future. The mail-order catalog provided people with an education in household technology. It created a market for innovative products and thus provided a spur for developing them.

Looking over an old catalog today is more than just an exercise in nostalgia. It can tell us a great deal about the way people lived—not about the great events of life, but about the ordinary day-to-day activities, which in the end make up most of life.

For example, in an introduction to a reprint of an 1895 Ward's catalog, Boris Emmet observes,

> According to the Dry Goods Department of the 1895 catalog, the housewife of the gay 90's was not gay; she was busy! She had the opportunity to make almost every item in her family's wardrobe. She could make her own sheets, weave her own carpets, quilt her own quilts, even sew tents for family camping trips.

There were only four pages of the nearly 600-page volume devoted to ladies' and girls' clothes. There were 31 pages of fabrics. Women were expected to make their own and their children's clothes. The housewife was urged to buy a full bolt of whatever cloth she desired because "it costs less when we don't have to unroll." If a full bolt was more than she needed, the customer was urged to sell or share the remainder with a neighbor.

There was a far, far larger selection of ready-to-wear

men's and boys' clothing. The lady of the house was urged to "insist upon it that the men of your family dress well provided they do so without increased cost." A top-line Ward's suit in 1890 went for about $28.

The catalog contained a large selection of jewelry, not because people wore more jewelry, but because jewelry was not the sort of thing the housewife could make at home. If she wanted it, she had to buy it ready-made.

In contrast, today's catalogs contain more pages of women's and girls' clothing than of anything else. The woman of the house is no longer expected to sew her own clothes.

While Montgomery Ward's was the pioneer and leader in mail-order selling to the end of the nineteenth century, it was ultimately knocked out of the top spot in that field by a younger, more aggressive rival, Sears, Roebuck and Co.

Sears, Roebuck was basically the brainchild of a hungry young mail-order salesman named Richard W. Sears. In 1887, the 23-year-old Sears was selling watches by mail order from Chicago. Business was good, and Sears began looking around for a skilled watchmaker who could repair the products that he sold. He advertised for one, and Alvah C. Roebuck responded. The men became partners, but Roebuck was never really more than a good watch repairman and never played an active part in managing the company. In the early years Sears, Roebuck was entirely a Richard Sears show.

Richard Sears knew, as had Montgomery Ward, that nineteenth-century America was basically a rural society. Three-quarters of the people lived on farms. But unlike the peasants of Europe and Asia, the American farmers were relatively prosperous and becoming more so. They were also not bound by hundreds of years of tradition and had eagerly accepted the new tools for farming that were the products of the industrial revolution. The corn shucker, the mechanical harvester, the cream separator, and many other new pieces of farm machinery were rapidly incorporated into the farmers' working life, and these helped to increase their efficiency and add greatly to their prosperity. Late nineteenth-century American farmers were potentially marvelous customers. They could accept innovation, and by and large they could afford it. The only problem was getting the products to the farmers and their families.

Sears was more of a swashbuckler than Ward. The Ward's catalog tended to provide a picture of an item accompanied by a fairly straightforward description of that item. Ward's described its Grand Windsor Range thus:

> We make this range with sufficient flue capacity for soft coal, and with properly constructed fire boxes, flue plates and damper arrangements to be durable.
>
> We can furnish fixtures for the Grand Windsor Range (any size), which include front and bottom grates, at an extra charge of $1.00. We do not furnish any cooking utensils, stove boards, or the first joint of pipe, with any of our ranges at the prices quoted.

A nearly identical stove offered by Sears was touted under the headline "OUR NEW 1901 MODEL ACME PRINCESS COOK STOVE." Customers were then told, "We offer the Acme Princess as an entirely new stove for 1901, made in our own foundry from the best material that money can buy, by the most skilled mechanics that we can employ." Every feature of the Sears stove was described with exaggeration. The flues were "very large," the materials "extra heavy," and the stove was designed so that somehow the user could avoid "all possibility of spilling ashes on the floor while cleaning the stove," an impossible claim.

Sears knew he was exaggerating, but he said it was the only way to attract people's attention.

The early Sears catalog was aggressively folksy. Sears called his catalog "the farmer's friend." It read not so much like a catalog as a personal letter. The catalog's first task was to break through the farmer's fear and suspicion of big city merchants. Sears headquarters was in Chicago, a place that Iowa farmers had heard of but not seen. And what the farmer heard was not too good. "Don't be afraid that you will make a mistake," Sears wrote at the beginning of one of his early catalogs. "We receive hundreds of orders every day from young and old who never before sent away for goods. We are accustomed to handling all kinds of orders. Tell us what you want in your own way, written in any language, no matter whether good or poor writing, and the goods will promptly be sent to you."

The Sears, Roebuck Company worked hard to make good on that pledge.

Both Sears and Ward's also pledged that if the customer was not satisfied, money would be refunded, and in general, that pledge seemed to be kept as well. There was a popular though perhaps apocryphal story about a customer who personally came to see Sears in Chicago with a watch that he had dropped on a rock in the mud. The watch had naturally suffered greatly by this accident. Sears immediately handed the man a replacement watch. The customer protested, saying that the damage was his fault. But, as the story goes, Sears said, "We guarantee our watches not to fall out of people's pockets and bounce in the mud."

Another statement popularly attributed to Sears is, "Honesty is the best policy, I have tried it both ways and I know."

The other and less attractive side of the Sears honesty policy can be seen in a Sears ad for an "UPHOLSTERED PARLOR SET of three pieces" for an astounding 195¢. Customers who sent for the set expecting to get something they could sit on would have been disappointed when they discovered that this was furniture that only a child's doll could sit on. True enough, the ad did contain the word "miniature" in smaller type. But there was also information on how the items had to be boxed and shipped, and a hasty reading would certainly give the impression that what was to be shipped was a full-sized upholstered parlor set. In dealing with such advertising, the old wisdom about "let the buyer beware" had to apply.

Another prominent feature of late nineteenth- and early twentieth-century catalogs that people today find surprising and even shocking are the extensive sections on drugs and patent medicines. Many farmers rarely saw a doctor. When they were ill, they relied on medicines from the store or the catalog. Everything was available. There were sure-cure pills for smoking and drinking and a liquid that would allow customers to break their opium or morphine habit (a habit they may well have acquired by using drug-laced patent medicines also sold by the mail-order companies). There were pills for heart trouble and asthma as well as "Our Famous Blood Pills, For men or women that require a nerve tonic, blood purifier or builder." Also for sale were "electric belts"—though the copy in the catalog did not quite say so, they were clearly meant to be male virility builders, "For nervous disease of all kind, weakness of any kind." The belt was also said to be good for headaches and backaches. The embarrassed customer was assured "we will send it in a plain sealed box so the express agent or no one else can tell the contents." Around the turn of the century, electricity still carried a magical aura for most people. They didn't understand what it could and could not do.

A host of laws—the Pure Food and Drug Act, as well as truth in advertising regulations—forced Sears and other mail-order merchants to clean up their act. Indeed, even before the laws began to close in, the Sears catalog had changed, cutting back on extravagant and misleading claims. Sears himself saw the need for the change in styles. He had always looked upon flamboyant advertising as a way to attract customers. Now he had them, and in order to retain the confidence of his customers, the catalog had to provide them with more accurate information. But Sears, who was basically a swashbuckling mail-order merchant, was never quite comfortable with his growing respectability. Gradually he turned over the management of the company and the writing of the catalog copy to others.

After the departure of Richard Sears from the scene, the Sears catalog became a less exciting, but no less popular, item to read. Gordon L. Weil wrote in his book *Sears, Roebuck, U.S.A.*, "If you grew up in rural America, you probably remember the Sears catalog with affection. The old edition of the big book frequently was hung in the outhouse, where it would provide essential reading material and where its pages could serve a more mundane but no less vital function."

A few years ago, reprints of old Sears catalogs hit the

best-seller list. But reading the mail-order catalog is not just a piece of history. The catalog is still very much with us today. America has changed. Now the vast majority of people live in cities and towns in easy reach of department stores or well-stocked suburban shopping malls. Merchandising has changed as well. Even Sears has changed. The popularity of mail-order shopping actually reached its height during the 1920s. The postal service had been expanding. Rural Free Delivery was established so farmers no longer had to go to the post office to mail their orders. The post office began delivering packages with its parcel post service in 1913, first for small packages and then, in order to accommodate the mail-order business, for larger and larger items. Small merchants objected to the postal changes, but the mail-order companies prevailed.

The good times for Sears and a lot of other companies ended in 1929 when the Great Depression began. Before the depression was over, American buying habits had changed again. People had stopped buying as much by mail and increasingly relied on the retail store. This was due as much to the change in the living patterns of Americans as it was to the depression. By the outbreak of World War II, the United States was no longer a predominantly rural country. Whereas once the majority of people had lived on isolated farms, the majority now lived in metropolitan areas or had easy access to them.

By that time, Sears was no longer strictly a mail-order house. It had begun to open retail outlets in the 1920s and, in the years that followed, had done an increasing volume of business through them. But it has never abandoned the catalog. The semiannual main catalog still averages over 1,300 pages. Photography has replaced the old woodcuts, and the patent medicines and electric belts are gone. The large section of farming equipment, everything from plows to baby chicks, is no longer included in the main catalog. Farmers can get a special supplementary catalog to meet their needs. There are also supplementary catalogs for offices, home repairs, automobile equipment, and other areas of special interest. There is a Christmas catalog of about 700 pages, which concentrates on toys and other Christmas gifts—it's called the Wish Book. But the main catalog still features everything from stoves to slippers.

Sears, along with Wards and now J. C. Penney, another retail giant that has entered the catalog field, relies more on telephone than mail-order sales. The customer phones in his or her order, which is then picked up by the customer at the store. That saves on shipping costs. People also use the catalog as a guide. After reading it over slowly at home and deciding what they want, they can then go down to the retail store and buy the item from stock.

So the mail-order merchants have survived the changes in America's buying habits, by adapting. Some like Sears have even prospered in the new atmosphere, though like other companies Sears has its ups and downs. While the present Sears catalog is as big and bulky as it ever was, it is no longer the magic book that it had been earlier in the century. For the catalog is no longer the isolated farm family's chief window onto a wider world. It is just another selling tool.

9

Getting Comfortable

IF YOU STEPPED into the living room of a solid middle-class home of one hundred years ago, the first thought that might strike you is, "My God, what a lot of pillows."

For many families a century ago, pillows were almost an obsession. There would be extra pillows on the already well stuffed sofa and chairs, pillows on the window seat, sometimes even pillows on the floor. These were usually for children to sit on.

And what a variety of shapes and colors. There were round pillows, square ones, flat ones, triangular ones, and cylindrical ones. Pillows were made in silk, plush, corduroy, or just about any other fabric available. And they came with and without fringes, tufts, ruffles, and buttons.

The pillow was more than something to sit on or prop your arm against. Pillows were used to add color to a room and also to make a personal statement about the owners of the house. A pillow was a way for a woman to display her sewing and embroidering skills conspicuously. Women's magazines were filled with designs for different sorts of pillows, and women spent many hours embroidering pillows with pictures, autographs, and mottoes. Pillows were also popular souvenirs. Visitors to distant cities or to the seashore often returned with pillows emblazoned with the name and sometimes a picture of the place they had visited. Pink "Souvenir of Niagara Falls" pillows could be found in the homes of many newlyweds one hundred years ago.

By the last decade of the nineteenth century, the really heavy and ornate furniture that had been the fashion in earlier years had begun to give way to somewhat simpler styles, though the furniture was still ornate and heavy by our standards.

In an earlier era, windows had been thickly curtained, partly to keep in the heat, but also to keep out sunlight, which faded upholstery fabrics. But colorfast fabrics became available, and the *Ladies' Home Journal* suggested that the living room contain "nothing that will be harmed by exposure to sun and light." The heavy curtains were banished. So too were the heavy rugs, which were so very hard to clean. The hardwood floors were often highly polished and covered with Chinese- or Japanese-style matting or an occasional throw rug. The throw rugs, by the way, were a menace on the polished floor; a careless step would send the rug flying and the stepper sprawling on his or her backside.

The furniture in the living room was to be, in the words of the *Ladies' Home Journal*, "of the most substantial and comfortable kind, with nothing too good for use." It was to contain at minimum a couch, a large table, several upholstered chairs, a bookcase, some pictures, very possibly a piano and good lighting.

Comfortable was a key word in the furnishings of that era. The living room of one hundred years ago was not quite the sort of place where you could kick off your shoes and put your feet up on the table. But when compared to the stiff formal parlors of the 1860s and 1870s, the living room of one hundred years ago was comfortable indeed. It was meant for living. People sat in the living room to read, to sew, or to talk. It was not a room to be used only on Sunday afternoons or when the family had visitors.

Technology had brought about changes in the bedroom. Indoor plumbing had eliminated the need for the chamber pot, which had been a standard feature in bedrooms. The washstand, which once held the chamber pot, was still there, however, for it was needed to hold a pitcher and bowl for washing. With only one bathroom in the house, it was usually convenient to wash up in the bedroom at least some of the time.

Central heating had eliminated the need for a fireplace. And since the bedroom now could be kept reliably warm, it could be used for more than sleeping. Chairs or even a desk might be found in the bedroom. The bedroom was on its way to becoming a place where people could work, read, or just sit.

The bed, of course, was still the centerpiece of the room. The bed of one hundred years ago was by today's standards a heavy and elaborate piece of furniture. The canopy had returned to favor in the more fashionable homes. At one time, canopies and bed curtains were used for warmth, but this was unnecessary in the centrally heated bedroom. A canopy bed one hundred years ago was just for show. Children and poorer people used simpler metal-frame beds.

Mattresses were soft, uncomfortably so by our standards. And they tended to sag and get lumpy. Ward's offered a mattress filled with sea moss. It was recommended for delicate or nervous persons for its "tonic effect." The sheets were white, and flat, and they had to be ironed. Bolsters, long cylindrical pillows, were widely used, and on the madeup bed could be tossed any number of occasional pillows that had not found a place in the living room.

Built-in closets were just becoming standard architectural features. So in most older homes one hundred years ago, even in those houses that had been modernized, the bedroom was likely to contain an enormous cabinet called a wardrobe, in which most clothes were hung.

A look at the catalogs of the day indicates that an extra bed must have been a valuable commodity around most homes. Lounges or bed lounges—a piece of furniture unknown in the modern house—were the most popular furniture items sold by both Ward's and Sears.

Ward's described its line of bed lounges thus:

> Bed lounges weigh about 125 lbs. and vary in length from 6 feet to 6 feet 6 in. All our bed lounges have a spring bed on both sides and make as comfortable a bed as one can wish for. They are strong and well made and are perhaps the most necessary convenience a family can have. We ship lounges with backs and legs taken off, otherwise the freight would be twice as much. Anyone can put them together in a few minutes time.

The cost for most bed lounges in 1890 was under $10.

Another popular item was the folding bed, a bed that could be lifted off the floor and folded into a large cabinet. The bed could be folded into a simple cabinet or combined with a wardrobe, making an enormous piece of furniture weighing nearly 600 pounds.

The hammock was a favorite item, not for sleeping really but for lazing around in the backyard. If a house happened to have a front porch, it was usually a place where one hung a swing, a large swing for adults, not the playground swing that is familiar today.

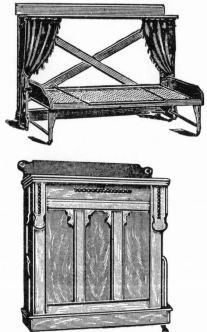

Folding beds offered in Montgomery Ward's 1895 catalog.

By the turn of the century, the furniture in the average home was moving toward greater simplicity. But the new styles did not please everyone. In her book of reminiscences, *Daddy Danced the Charleston*, Ruth Corbett recalls:

> Every few years there's an ugly period when taste is lost and grace of design is swallowed by garish, over-exaggerated form. You recall the disdain for Mid-Victorian gingerbread and furbelows. In the twenties and thirties none of us were contented until we had a set of "overstuffed," an understated name. The set consisted of a davenport, rocker and lounge chair—each sticking out its cheeks as if inflated and about to burst. Bristly mohair was a popular upholstery material. Sometimes the mohair or velour had cut designs or tapestry seats that would break the mohair monotony.

The profusion of pillows was gone, and so was the extreme clutter of the late-Victorian living room—but in general the living room furniture of the late twenties and thirties was not any more comfortable and practical than the living room furniture of an earlier era.

It was no easier to clean either, and many housewives turned to slipcovers to preserve the fabric of the over-stuffed furniture. The slipcovers could be taken off and washed, but they usually gave the couch or chair the appearance of a hippopotamus in an ill-fitting dress. Worse yet were the plastic slipcovers, which became popular with the rise of plastic after World War II. You could still sort of see the original surface of the furniture through the clear plastic cover, and such covers certainly did preserve the couch or chair. Anything spilled could be wiped off instantly. But, oh my, they were uncomfortable to sit on, hot and sticky in the summer, cold and clammy in the winter, and slippery year round.

To be fair, sofas with plastic covers were not really meant for sitting. The living room set was often the pride and joy of a poor family. It had cost them a great deal of money, and they wanted to preserve it, perhaps forever. In such a family, the living room was not really a place to sit anyway, except on very special and semiformal occasions. If you wanted to be comfortable, you went into the kitchen or bedroom. The living room was more of a museum, in which the family's proudest possessions, like the plastic-covered couch, were on display. Kids were regularly chased out of the living room.

The bedroom was simpler and less cluttered than before, primarily because the enormous wardrobe had been replaced by built-in closets, though for decades homeowners and apartment dwellers alike complained of lack of closet space. One of the great standing jokes of the radio comedians of the 1940s Fibber McGee and Molly was the hall closet. At least once during every show McGee would say he was going to the hall closet to get something. His wife Molly would exclaim, "Oh, no, not the hall closet!" The next thing you would hear was a tremendous series of crashes and rumbles, as all the objects that had been crammed into the hall closet came tumbling out. That moment always produced knowing laughter in the audience, most of whom had their version of the McGees' hall closet somewhere in their own home.

By the 1920s, the fashion for the canopied bed had died out, and beds became more austere and lighter. In the 1940s, there was what came to be known as the Hollywood bed, just a metal frame on wheels atop which was a set of box spring and mattress. A simple headboard might or might not be attached.

Electricity produced major changes in the way bedrooms were used. With the electric light, people could read in bed—that had been possible but difficult and a bit dangerous with a candle or oil lamp. Now it was easy and safe.

Keeping warm in bed had been a problem for centuries. In unheated bedrooms, cold was alleviated with bed warming pans, hot bricks, hot water bottles, and mounds of blankets. The electric blanket, another of the many items for the home that became popular after World War II, represented a genuine innovation in keeping warm at night. At first, there were fears of fire and shock with an electric blanket, but the blankets have turned out to be quite safe. Though electric blankets have never displaced conventional blankets for most of us, a substantial number of people today swear by them.

When television first entered the American home, it was in the living room or some other part of the house where the entire family gathered. But as families acquired two or three TV sets, they quickly made their way into the bedroom. Watching TV from bed is now an established custom.

Early in the twentieth century, a variation of the bed that folded into a wardrobe became popular in hotels, rooming houses, and small apartments. It was called among other things the "in-a-door-bed," because it folded into a niche in the wall that was then covered by a door. It was also called a Murphy bed because a popular version of the bed had been invented by a man named Murphy. The

Murphy bed that would swing up or down unpredictably, often trapping some poor fellow inside it when it was closed, was a popular prop in early screen comedies.

The Murphy bed is relatively rare now, and today the extra bed is generally provided by the convertible sofa, a piece of furniture in which the bed folds out of a conventional-looking couch.

For centuries, couples had been sleeping in double beds. But starting in the 1930s, Hollywood censors decreed that it was immoral to show two people, even if they were supposed to be a married couple, together in a bed. So bedroom scenes had people sleeping in two separate beds.

The modern convertible sofa. (Castro Convertibles)

These beds were often placed a considerable distance from one another, perhaps with a bed table between them. People did not live that way, but the influence of Hollywood was so great that a lot of people began to believe that what they saw on the screen was an accurate reflection of reality. Married couples began buying twin beds just like the ones they saw in the movies.

The twin bed has disappeared from the movies, except perhaps on the late late show. It has also generally disappeared from the bedrooms of America. The trend has been toward larger beds—queen-sized, king-sized, even round beds. And then there is the water bed—one of the few truly revolutionary changes in bedroom furniture of the past one hundred years. Oh, yes, there are now beds that can be raised or lowered at the touch of a button, but these are mere adaptations of the hospital bed. And there are beds that vibrate—but these are gimmicks. The water bed is truly innovative. Instead of sleeping on springs and stuffing, you sleep atop what is basically a big plastic bag filled with heated water. Sleeping on a water bed feels a bit like sleeping on warm Jell-O. When water beds were first introduced to the general public in the 1960s, they were considered bizarre and somehow immoral. While they have never replaced the standard mattress and do not seem destined to do so, they have become respectable. Use of water beds is no longer limited to the young and *avant-garde*. They have become increasingly popular among the old, who find that the warm feeling and silent rippling motion of the water eases some of the aches and pains of age.

10

The
Home as a Dream

MOVE TO THE suburbs. Get away from the crowds, the dirt, and the crime of the city. Raise your family in a healthy, clean environment where the children can be close to nature.

Does that sound familiar? It should. That is what suburban builders and many suburban homeowners say to people who live in or near the city. They have been saying pretty much the same thing for a long time, at least a hundred years. Fear and even hatred of the city, coupled with a desire to move out to a home "in the country," are permanent fixtures of the American mental landscape.

For many Americans, the idea of a home can evoke an almost religious fervor. "Home," wrote a nineteenth-century New York builder in one of his advertisements, "what tender associations and infinite meanings cluster around that blessed word." A bit sentimentally stated for our taste perhaps, but many people would basically agree with that statement.

Owning one's own home has always been a part, a big part, of what is called the American Dream.

The lure of a home in the suburbs began after the Civil War and reached its nineteenth-century peak during the 1880s and 1890s. The technological development that made a move to the suburbs possible in 1890 was the streetcar. In her book *Building the Dream*, Gwendolyn Wright points out that up until about the 1870s public transportation was limited to the horsecar, which was slow, and the railroad train, which was expensive and didn't run very often. Starting in the early 1880s, the electric railway, what later became known as the streetcar, began to make its appearance in cities throughout the United States.

In 1910 the streetcar was an important means of transportation, but it wasn't perfect. (Frank Wing of the *Minneapolis Journal*)

The electric streetcar gained immediate acceptance, and by 1890, over fifty cities had streetcar lines. Five years later, the number had jumped to 850 cities. Streetcars not only connected various parts of a city, they ran well into the country and connected nearby cities with one another. Says Wright,

> "Streetcar suburbs" sprang up along all these routes. On Sundays, free excursion cars often decked out with banners, flags and a brass band, would take the crowds of potential buyers out to the open fields where they might purchase their suburban home. Subdividers promised the felicitous unity of urban comforts and rustic simplicity, progress and nostalgia that characterized the ideal American community.

Being close to "nature," that is, living outside of the city, was believed to be both physically healthy and morally uplifting. Therefore, the late-nineteenth-century suburbs tried to project an image of being "natural." The advertising put out by the developers, as well as the drawings that appeared in magazines, pictured the typical suburban house of a century ago as being surrounded by trees and a wide lawn. In truth, most of the houses were built on flat barren sites with little or no natural greenery. The trees had all been cut down to make room for the houses. Except for the most expensive of them, the suburbs of a century ago were built without sidewalks or paved streets. Drainage and sewers were often haphazardly provided for and were a constant worry. There were few planned parks or other public amenities for the average resident of a streetcar suburb.

People were willing to overlook the multiple incon-

The suburban dream house of 1905 could be built for under $2,400. (New York Public Library Picture Collection)

veniences to fulfill their dream of a home. For the man, the home was supposed to be a refuge from the harried and often cutthroat activity of the business world. The home was also supposed to be a place that sheltered both women and children from the harshness and evil influence of city life. For the wives in many poorer families that had just managed to scrape together enough to buy a house, the suburbs may have seemed a paradise of sorts. Many women had worked in factories or done laundry before their marriage and move to the suburbs.

Then, as now, the city had a bad reputation. In truth, one hundred years ago the living conditions in large parts of many cities were absolutely awful.

One hundred years ago, the cities of America were being transformed by waves of immigration from southern and eastern Europe. The bulk of the immigrants were Catholics and Jews. Blacks from the South were arriving in northern cities in unprecedented numbers, and in California there were large influxes of Chinese and Japanese. Then, as now, some of the flight of the white Protestant middle-class to the suburbs was due to prejudice. Most of the immigrants were poor and unskilled, and they had to live in the central cities, close to the small businesses and factories where they found jobs. Indeed, many were prevented by law, as well as custom, from living or owning property outside of well-defined ghetto districts.

In the cities, immigrants moved into structures that either were converted from warehouses, small factories, or private homes into multiple-unit dwellings, or were buildings specially constructed to provide cheap housing. In either case, the conditions under which people were forced to live were quite horrifying. When the writer Charles Dickens, who was used to the slums of London, visited the notorious New York neighborhood known as Five Points, he found it filled with "all that was loathesome, drooping and decayed."

The following quotation, which comes from the Yiddish newspaper the *Daily Forward* in 1905, describes what it was like for many recent Jewish immigrants living on New York's Lower East Side. Similar living conditions existed among newly arrived Italians, blacks, Chinese, and others:

> Everybody knows the facts about the terrible poverty in immigrant families. The following data are

excerpts from the official medical report of the New York Lying-In Hospital.

Here is our doctor at the door of an apartment in 120 Delancy Street. The family arrived in America six weeks ago, the mother just gave birth to her first child. The father is an unemployed painter. The two-room apartment is occupied by the father, mother, newborn child, and eight boarders. Can you imagine the horror and debasement of giving birth in the presence of eight strangers? The mother lies on an old sofa and there are piles of dirt in all the corners. The boarders sleep on old mattresses.

68 Moore Street. This is the mother's seventh child. The family of nine lives in one room, of which the front part is the father's shoemaking "business." Here he plies his trade. The single window is also the show window. The room is indescribably filthy. The parents look to the time when the oldest boy will be twelve and go to work.

166 Norfolk St. The happy parents welcome their first child. They live in a furnished room, together with two other couples. There is only one bed. When the doctor asks where they sleep, they can only reply that they manage somehow. The doctor thinks they take turns, each night a different couple uses the bed. Or perhaps on an hourly schedule: One couple has the bed till midnight, then it goes to the other.

The horrors of ghetto life in the city began to become an issue in America about one hundred years ago. Social reformers who had visited the slums were writing and publishing reports on what they had seen. Statistical studies revealed an alarming rate of disease and crime among the tenement dwellers.

More impressive than either the written reports or the statistics were photographs. By the turn of the century, it had become possible to reproduce photographs on a mass scale. The technology of photography had improved to the point where photographers could leave their studios and take pictures not only in the streets, but with the aid of a flash, in the dark crowded hallways and cramped rooms of the tenements themselves. People living in the relative ease and comfort of the suburbs could see what life was really like for the poor.

By far the most effective of all the photojournalists of the slums was Danish-born Jacob Riis. For years, he prowled the streets and back alleys of New York City, producing devastating and heartbreaking photos of *How the Other Half Lives*, which was also the title of his most famous book. Words and statistics might be overlooked; Riis's photographs and those taken by other muckraking photojournalists could not. Riis and the others concentrated on the housing conditions—the tenement building itself was viewed as the source of evil. If people could just be given better housing, the theory of the time ran, then many of the problems associated with slum living would disappear.

Disease in the slums was a major source of concern. One hundred years ago, the germ theory of disease was just beginning to penetrate public consciousness. Sanitary conditions in the slums were notorious and the rate of disease frighteningly high. There developed a widespread public fear that epidemics might spread from the slums and infect the entire city and even the suburbs. There was an

The slums of New York City as photographed by Jacob Riis.
(New York Public Library Picture Collection)

additional fear. It arose from the piecework system. Many tenement dwellers did piecework in their apartments. It was a common practice for families to take in "homework" from small businesses and subcontractors. Tailoring, cigar making, and the making of paper flowers and other small ornaments could be done with a few simple tools in the home—and everybody in the family except the very small children could and did participate. (Many tiny apartments were part workshop as well.) The fear was that products made in disease-ridden tenement apartments could be contaminated and spread the disease among buyers.

In truth, many of the fears of epidemics or contaminated products appear to have been exaggerated, but those involved in social reform emphasized such possibilities as a means of getting the more affluent concerned about the plight of the poor. People were being told that if they did not do something about the slums, the diseases that festered in the tenements would strike them and their families.

Attempts were made to redesign the tenement building into something that was both profitable and more livable. One of the greatest criticisms of tenement buildings in New York City was that in most only the front and rear rooms had windows. The buildings were constructed right up against one another so that there was no place for side windows except in corner buildings. The apartments inside such buildings were called railroad flats because the rooms ran in straight lines like railroad cars. In such a building, there were four apartments to a floor, two front and two back. For the front apartment, the parlor overlooked the street. It was the only room with windows. Behind the parlor was a kitchen and two or three bedrooms. The rear apartment was arranged in the reverse order with the parlor windows overlooking a tiny backyard. Not only was such an arrangement stuffy and cheerless, in case of fire the windowless rooms were death traps.

In response to criticism, new tenements were designed a bit differently into what came to be known as the dumbbell shape. The building was thicker at each end than in the middle. The sides of the dumbbell building were indented slightly, so that there was enough space for windows in the interior rooms. These windows did not look out over a street or yard, but into a narrow air shaft between one tenement and the next.

Architects and social reformers complained that the

dumbbell tenement represented only a tiny improvement over the old railroad flat. But since the building did meet the minimum standards of a new housing law in New York, it quickly became the prevailing model for the new tenement. Thousands of them were built during the last two decades of the nineteenth century. Tenement dwellers were fond of saying that the building provided the maximum profit for the owner with the maximum discomfort for the tenant. These "model" tenements soon became notorious.

The air shafts, which were supposed to provide light and air for inside rooms, became places where tenants on the upper floors often threw their garbage. Tenement dwellers were not just dirty or lazy. It was neither easy nor safe to maneuver the narrow, generally unlighted stairs with a load of garbage that was to be taken to the street.

There were shops with rooms behind them on the lower floor. The upper floors had two 4-room apartments in the front and two 3-room apartments in the rear. Seven-by-eight-foot bedroom alcoves stood between the kitchen and a parlor bedroom. In the public hallway opposite the stairs were one or two toilets and a sink.

In 1893, over a million New Yorkers, 70 percent of the population at that time, lived in multiple-family dwellings, four-fifths of which were tenements. The majority of these tenements were of the dumbbell variety. After the turn of the century, it became illegal to construct new dumbbell tenements—but even today many of these old buildings are still in use.

While the dumbbell tenement was peculiar to New York City, other cities had other types of tenement dwellings—most of these had been converted from single-family dwellings. But such structures rarely represented any sort of improvement in housing for the poor.

There were genuine attempts to improve housing for the urban poor. A number of fairly successful model tenements were built. But they remained isolated experiments because of economics—such buildings could not be operated as profitably as other tenements. There was no government subsidy for housing until the 1930s.

In the years that followed World War II, there was a wave of "slum clearance" in many cities. Tenements and other rundown buildings were demolished in great numbers and replaced by newer, better types of housing and other structures. Slum clearance often improved an area and some people made a lot of money, but the basic problem of where to house the former slum dwellers remained. Often they just moved into bad housing in other areas, thus creating new slums.

By the 1940s, the idea that the government should do something to provide adequate housing for the poor had taken hold in America, and there were a large number of public housing projects built. In addition to projects completely financed by the government, there were also many types of partially subsidized low-income housing.

Public housing has not been an unqualified success in America. Many of the projects quickly became as rundown and dangerous as the tenement buildings they had been designed to replace. Some projects became so bad that they had to be demolished. Public housing projects often created a variety of difficult and complicated social problems for the neighborhoods in which they were placed. Many of the public housing residents themselves resented the way in which housing planners and government officials attempted to control their lives.

By the late 1960s, public housing had gotten such a bad name in America that people had to be reminded of two things. First, not all public housing has failed; there are some successful and stable projects. Second, although public housing didn't solve the housing problems of the poor, it didn't create them either. The "good old days" were the days of the dumbbell tenement. The problems of housing for the poor are not new, and they are still with us.

Small wonder that a house in the suburbs was a dream for millions of Americans one hundred years ago and has remained a dream for many up to the present day.

Still, not every multiple-residence dwelling was a tenement slum, and not everyone dreamed of a home in the suburbs. Indeed, as time went on, technology made the apartment building a more attractive place to live. A century ago, hot and cold running water and indoor plumbing were still luxuries in most private homes, but they were standard in the better class of apartment building. There were central gas mains for lighting and central switchboards that could connect telephone calls at any hour, and of course, there was central heating. Newer apartment buildings contained elevators, an enormous boon to apartment living, for tenants no longer had to climb four or five flights of stairs. With elevators, taller apartment buildings could be constructed. That represented a more economical use of limited city land. Some apartment buildings even had central vacuum cleaning systems. As the use of electricity became practical, it was the apartment house that was electrified first. Often apartment houses jumped the gun on public utilities by installing their own generators.

Still, despite the many advantages of apartments, Americans have never been entirely comfortable with them. Around the turn of the century, apartment buildings, no matter how technologically advanced and even luxurious they might have been, were still associated with the horrible tenements that had become the symbol of all that was evil about urban life. Apartment buildings, where people lived in close proximity to one another, were regarded as places in which immorality would thrive. The relative ease of housekeeping in apartments led some critics to fear that they would cause women to neglect their traditional wifely duties and thus lead to a breakup of the American family. Finally, many Americans were upset by apartments just because apartment living had long been popular in Europe, particularly in France, and American apartment dwellers seemed somehow to be adopting "decadent" European life-styles.

These various moral objections and qualms were overridden by economic necessity. Cities were growing and people needed places to live. Not everyone could afford a home in the suburbs, and not everybody wanted one with its long trolley ride to the central city where most people worked. Land in central city areas was so expensive that the apartment building was the only practical solution. Besides some people liked the convenience of the apartment.

The complaints about city life continued, and there was a constant refrain which held that Americans should abandon the city and go back to the pure life of the farm or the small town. Each new technical advance was looked upon as a possible way of getting people out of the immoral city. Take the attitude expressed toward the spread of electrical power.

In 1929, the business writer Waldemar Kaempffert wrote,

> Power is no longer confined. Already we are immersed in a vast, unseen ocean of it that can be tapped by the farmhouse or steel mill. Industry is responding. No longer is the huge city, with its swarming hordes lodged in tenements, its huddled factories, its disgraceful subways and street cars, to dominate society. Industry is migrating or establishing itself anew in the small town. The current of emigration which has been steadily flowing to the city for decades is now flowing back to the country. Unlike the first industrial revolution the age of superpower, of energy shot with the speed of light into thousands of small towns and villages, was foreseen . . . engineers began to plan the second electrical revolution—the revolution which was to free energy from time and space.

Kaempffert's predictions were written at an unfortunate moment—1929 was the year of the stock market crash and it marked the start of the Great Depression. The depression didn't really end for the United States until the country entered World War II in 1941. Though electrical power had certainly moved from the big city to the countryside, there was no great exodus of people from the cities back to the country and small towns. Indeed, the trend of moving into the cities continued and was accelerated by the war. After the war, however, another major move to the suburbs began. The spur for the new move out from the

Suburbia in the early 1930s. (New York Public Library Picture Collection)

cities was not electrical power as Kaempffert had predicted, but the automobile.

In the 1880s and 1890s, suburbs had grown up along streetcar lines and later along commuter rail lines. But the suburbanite had to live close to a trolley stop or train station. That severely limited suburban spread. With the car, no such proximity to public transportation was necessary—the suburbs could expand practically anywhere there was a road, and if there was no road, one could be built.

Automobiles had been increasingly popular on the American scene since the 1920s—but the real explosion in automobile traffic came in the years following World War II. At that time, America was more prosperous than it had ever been, and the dream of practically every Amer-

162

ican family was to own a car. With that car, Father could
drive from his home in the suburbs to his job in the city
or at least to the train station. For many there was more
than a dream involved. There had been virtually no housing construction in the United States during World
War II. When the war ended, thousands upon thousands
of servicemen returned to their families or married as they
had planned to do. But they found they had no place to
live. Families doubled and tripled up. For many Americans
who had come through the rigors of the war years sustained

World War II created an enormous housing shortage. Here
newcomers to San Francisco in 1943 line up at a War Housing
Center, hoping a house or apartment will be available for them.
(Office of War Information photo)

"Now let's see, there's Mr. and Mrs. Falk and their youngest daughter plus their son Harry with his wife and two children, together with their married daughter Edna, her husband and baby, not to forget old Grandma Falk."

1946 cartoon lampooning the post-World War II housing shortage. Santa is trying to deliver presents to a family still living in a "temporary" quonset hut. (*The Saturday Review*)

by the dream of a home of their own, living with in-laws was more like a nightmare.

Many former barracks and other military buildings, including the semicircular, corrugated metal structures called Quonset huts, were converted into "temporary" veterans' housing. Some veterans and their families found themselves living in such "temporary" housing five years or more after the war had ended.

During the early 1950s, the prefabricated house became the rage. These were houses in which most of the major parts—the walls, the roof, the windows, the ceilings, and so forth—were produced in factories. The premade or prefabricated parts were then shipped to the site and put together, sometimes within a matter of hours. Many of the techniques of prefabrication were developed during the war years. The prefabricated house seemed a solution to the acute housing shortage. Companies that built them were widely advertised and supported by government loans and tax breaks. The prefabricated house was better than the Quonset hut (which was also prefabricated), but it was not quite the American Dream either. Often such houses were poorly made, doors and windows did not fit properly, ceilings leaked, walls were paper thin. From being hailed as a solution to the housing shortage, the prefabricated house became something of a sour joke, a synonym for poor housing. Besides, they were not as cheap or as easy to build as first thought. Prefabricated housing was a basically good idea, but it had been oversold.

More successful was the approach used by developers who employed a combination of prefabricated materials and conventional building techniques. Of these builders, the most successful of all was Levitt and Sons. Between 1947 and 1951, the company built 17,450 houses in Levittown, Long Island. What had been a potato field at the end of World War II became a community of 75,000 people, all living in new Levitt-constructed homes. So successful was the Long Island development that the firm went on to build Levittowns in other parts of the country.

Levitt gave people what most surveys said they wanted: houses with traditional styling but containing all the modern conveniences. Besides the basic house, Levitt also provided refrigerators, washing machines, dryers, built-in television sets, air conditioners, and many other modern appliances. The Levitt house was sold completely decorated. All the new owner had to do was move in the furniture. In addition, the Levitt developments often had swimming pools and community centers. Levitt was not just selling houses. He was selling a way of life. Other developers tried to imitate the Levitt success formula. Though there was a lot of snickering about the uniformity of Levittown and other suburban developments, they were what a large segment of the American population had dreamed of. A survey taken by the magazine *Saturday Evening Post* at the end of World War II indicated that the vast majority of the American public—some 85 percent —did not want to live in an apartment or a "used house." They wanted a new house built with all the modern conveniences. They wanted a large picture window in their house, a barbecue pit outside, and a well-mowed lawn. In the suburbs, the power mower became a status symbol, though many of the lawns were barely large enough to require them.

The suburbs as typified by Levittown was the post–World War II American Dream. For many people, born long after World War II ended, that dream is still alive.

11

The Future

It's CRYSTAL BALL time. Predicting the future of household technology (or anything else for that matter) is a hazardous business, for so many predictions turn out not only to be wrong, but they also make the prophet look foolish.

Take the push-button kitchen. In the 1940s, there were all sorts of predictions that in the "kitchen of the future" all one would have to do is push a button and a fully prepared meal would be delivered, hot from the oven —no extra preparation required. It is true that your microwave oven can present you with soggy Swiss steak and a couple of mouthfuls of tasteless mashed potatoes in just a few minutes. All you have to do is put the frozen dinner in the oven and push a few buttons. But that is not the mouth-watering and elaborate push-button dinner that had been dreamed of. That was a prophecy gone wrong. In fact, since the 1940s, there has been a trend to gourmet cooking, and that kind of cooking takes more time than ever. So much for "the kitchen of the future."

There was another popular 1940s prediction—the house would be cleaned by a robot. Well, we don't have any house-cleaning robots, and there are no prospects for getting any in the near future. The motions required for such acts as dusting and vacuuming are too complex and varied for even the most sophisticated robots now available or contemplated. Machines are better at mathematics than mopping.

With those words of caution out of the way, we can now plunge ahead and try to predict what changes are going to take place in the home over the next hundred years. Let's start with some fairly obvious trends.

Whatever it is that will heat and power the house over the next century, the fuel almost certainly will not be oil. The age of oil is on its way out. The oil crisis of the 1970s marked a very real and profound change in the way all of us live. There had long been warnings about an energy crisis, but the warnings did not strike home until the 1970s. The price of fuel and electricity shot up. It was no longer cheap to heat your home or turn on your air conditioner. It wasn't cheap to drive to work either.

Recently the price of oil has not been rising quite as fast as it had during the late 1970s. Indeed, it has even gone down a bit. But don't deceive yourself, oil will never be cheap again. Politics aside, the world is simply running out of oil and natural gas; there is no possible way that we can continue to use these fuels at the current rate for another hundred years or even another fifty. New energy sources must be found.

In 1950 or even 1960, it would have been reasonable

to predict that in the future much of the world's power would be supplied by nuclear reactors. It is no longer safe to predict that nuclear energy is the wave of the future. Nuclear reactors are turning out not to be nearly as reliable as predicted; and they are far, far more expensive to operate than had been estimated. There is a genuine fear that nuclear reactors are not safe. Many Americans just don't trust nuclear power.

So unless there are some important technological advances and a change in public attitude toward nuclear power, where is the energy going to come from? It most certainly will come from somewhere. Perhaps it will be some sort of synthetic fuel now being tested in the laboratory. Or perhaps the house of the future will have huge panels on the roof to collect solar energy. Or there may be a gigantic windmill in the front yard of many homes. Whatever will happen, it is clear that the home of the near future, at least, is going to be built with a great deal more energy consciousness than was done with the home of the near past. We are already returning to many patterns of energy conservation that were more prevalent a century ago than thirty years ago.

There is another commodity that is likely to be in increasingly short supply in the future—fresh water. Americans have been as profligate in their use of water as they have been in their use of energy. The results can be seen in the many parts of the country that suffer from chronic shortages of fresh water. That may produce a shift away from the water-hungry well-mowed lawn. When landscaping a house, we will have to think more about plants that do not require so much water. Inside the house, cooking and washing cannot be done without water—though water-saving additions to showers have already been introduced in water-short communities. But what about the flush toilet? It is a great water waster, and it has only been around for about a century. It may not survive the next one hundred years. The flush toilet may be replaced by some sort of chemical toilet or by some variation of the old earth closet in areas where water is scarce.

These are fairly easy predictions, based on well-established and irreversible trends. There is going to be less fresh water in the world in one hundred years than there is today—unless there is some major technological breakthrough in converting seawater. There is certainly going to be less oil or natural gas. But when we get beyond these trends and venture into areas that involve human fashion and taste, prediction becomes more uncertain. But let's try a bit.

Will the private home in America survive the next one hundred years at all? At this point in history, private homes are in big trouble. They are very expensive to purchase and maintain and prohibitively expensive for many, many people. There have been suggestions that the private home will be entirely replaced by apartments, condominiums, or some other form of living arrangement. Well perhaps, but the desire for a "home of your own" runs very deep in America. I suspect a lot of people will somehow manage to buy private homes, no matter what the difficulties.

Clothes, furniture, the house in general will be easier to clean and care for in the next one hundred years. This will come about not so much through the development of new materials or techniques of cleaning, but through the development of materials that are easier to clean and keep clean. The coated water-resistant fabrics now used on much upholstery and the easy-care, no-iron clothes that most of us now wear may just be the harbingers of even tougher and easier-to-care-for fabrics of the future.

A century from now most people may still be sleeping on spring and fabric mattresses just as they do today, and just as they did one hundred years ago. But they may also be sleeping on water beds or on air cushions, which suspend the sleeper above the floor in much the same way as a hovercraft is suspended above the waves. Air cushion beds are technically possible now, though there has been no great consumer demand for them.

The greatest changes in the home over the next one hundred years will not come in what we sit on or sleep on or how we cook and store our food—the great changes will come through the television set, the home video game, and particularly the video game's big brother, the home computer.

The TV set has already changed the way we live. It keeps us at home for more of our entertainment—no need to go out to a movie or a baseball game. With larger numbers of channels available and with larger and more sophisticated sets and video recorders, this stay-at-home trend can be expected to continue. A century or less from now, we may have television screens that surround us rather than just sit in front of us. Holography, a process of three-dimensional photography that is now being developed, may be adapted to television, and instead of watching the characters of our favorite show, we will be able to feel as if we can actually walk among them. How about rooms or cabinets that can create a total environment through the senses of sight, sound, smell, even touch.

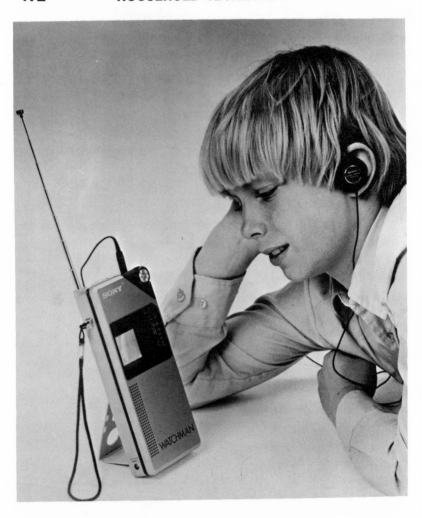

New technology will allow the development of flat pocket TV sets, such as this tiny, two-inch-screen Watchman from Sony. In the future the TV will be a more ubiquitous part of the home than ever before. (Sony Corporation of America)

Sound fantastic? Well perhaps—but is it any more fantastic than today's giant screen TV would have seemed to one who had used only the stereoscope? What many of us now call the TV room in the house is going to be a great deal more than that over the next century.

The changes that will be brought about by the home computer are even more far-reaching. The TV set is essentially passive. You watch it and react to what you see on the screen—the figures on the screen do not react to you. With the computer, there can be two-way communication. The video and computer games that are now popular will become more sophisticated.

You can ask the computer for information stored in its memory, and if your home computer is hooked up to a terminal that connects it with a network of other computers, it can call up information stored in the memory of distant computers. The home computer is just now becoming popular, and the computer terminal in a private home is still rare—but it is already part of many, many business offices.

As computers are brought into the home, it will be possible for more and more people to do more and more work in their own homes. What reason is there to go down to the office to look at a set of files when, with punching a few buttons, the necessary information will be displayed to you on a screen or printed out by your home computer. Over the next one hundred years when transportation may be more difficult and expensive because of congestion and the increasing cost of energy, working at home should become increasingly popular. Why fight the crowds on the freeway for an hour when you can do the same amount of work without ever leaving your house?

If people can work from their homes, then where

their homes are located will not be such a critical matter. The commuter who now resents traveling two hours a day to get to and from work may find the idea of traveling three or four hours once or twice a week a more attractive alternative.

Computers can do lots of other things; for example, in some places people can already shop with them. They can ask for an item to be displayed on the screen, express their willingness to buy, and actually arrange for a transfer of funds by punching a few buttons. Montgomery Ward and Richard Sears would have loved the system—it beats the old-fashioned catalog.

And what about the telephone, a subject barely discussed in this book, because it was invented more than one hundred years ago? Basically the home telephone has remained unaltered since its early days. There has been an improvement in the speed of getting calls through and in the quality of sound, and most important of all, you can reach practically anyone because practically everyone has a telephone. Still, talking on the telephone has remained one disembodied voice communicating with another disembodied voice. Video phones have been experimented with for years, and they were often demonstrated at science museums and industrial exhibits. But the practical video phone is now moving into offices. Can the home be far behind?

When you can not only talk to but see practically anyone from your own home, why go out?

All of these developments—TV, computer, and telephone will tend to make life over the next one hundred years more home-centered than it was during the past one hundred years. The possible implications of this development for society at large are staggering. Just one possible example of change brought about by an increasingly home-centered life would be an accelerated decline in the use of the automobile. The automobile, which really dominated American society for some fifty years, is already in decline —gas is expensive, roads are crowded, the fun has gone out of driving. If people no longer have to drive to work as often, or go shopping or visiting or to a movie, they will use their cars less often. There will be less of a need for new roads or shopping centers or parking lots.

But as was said at the beginning of this chapter, it is a very hazardous business to try to predict what homes will be like over the next century. The development of technology has proved to be erratic, and human tastes and fashions are even less predictable. It is entirely possible that in the future a person will sit at home in front of his or her life-sized three-dimensional TV set, waiting for the video phone to buzz or for a signal from the computer that the calculations he or she requested have been completed. But amid all those technical marvels, he or she may be sitting on an imitation mohair Victorian sofa, looking very much like the sofa found in homes one hundred years ago.

Bibliography

Armstrong, Hamilton F. *Those Days*. New York: Harper & Row, Publishers, 1963.

Boylan, James. *The World of the Twenties*. New York: Dial Press, 1973.

Conot, Robert. *A Streak of Luck*. New York: Seaview Books, 1979.

Corbett, Ruth. *Daddy Danced the Charleston*. Cranbury, N.J.: A. S. Barnes, 1970.

Giedion, Siegfried. *Mechanization Takes Command*. New York: W. W. Norton & Co., 1948.

Grosis, Leslie. *Housewife's Guide to Antiques*. New York: Exposition Press, 1959.

Howe, Irving, and Libo, Kenneth. *How We Lived*. New York: Richard Marek Publishers, 1979.

Jensen, Oliver; Kerr, Joan P.; and Belsky, Murray. *American Album*. New York: American Heritage, 1968.

Josephson, Matthew. *Edison*. New York: McGraw-Hill Book Co., 1959.

Quennell, Marjorie, and Quennell, C. H. A *History of Everyday Things in England*. London: B. T. Batsford, 1918.

Sears, Stephen W.; Belsky, Murray; and Tunsfell, Douglas. *Hometown, U.S.A.* New York: American Heritage, 1975.

Sloat, Warren. *1929: America Before the Crash*. New York: Macmillan, 1979.

Stewart, George R. *American Ways of Life*. New York: Doubleday & Co., 1954.

Sullivan, Mark. *Our Times: The United States 1900–1925*. New York: Charles Scribner's Sons, 1926.

Time-Life Book Editors. *This Fabulous Century: 1900–1910*. New York: Time-Life Books, 1964.

Walker, Robert H. *Everyday Life in the Age of Enterprise*. New York: G. P. Putnam's Sons, 1967.

Weil, Gordon L. *Sears, Roebuck, U.S.A.* New York: Stein & Day, Publishers, 1978.

Weisberger, Bernard A., and the editors of *Life. The Age of Steel and Steam*. New York: Time-Life Books, 1964.

Wilk, Max. *The Golden Age of Television*. New York: Delacorte Press, 1976.

Wright, Gwendolyn. *Building the Dream*. New York: Pantheon Books, 1981.

Index